W9-CNC-179

Tales from Penn State Football

BY KEN RAPPOPORT

Sports Publishing L.L.C

www.sportspublishingllc.com

Director of production: Susan M. Moyer
Project manager: Tracy Gaudreau
Developmental editor: Gabe Rosen
Copy editor: Cindy McNew and Susan M. Moyer
Dust jacket design: Joseph Brumleve
All photos courtesy of The Penn State University Archives

ISBN: 1-58261-405-9

Printed in the United States

Sports Publishing L.L.C.
www.sportspublishingllc.com

To my future stars:
Griffin, Camryn, Kayla, Adina and Shayna.

CONTENTS

ACKNOWLEDGMENTS

My thanks to Penn State sports information director Jeff Nelson for generously contributing vital information for this book. Also thanks to Lou Prato for his hospitality at Penn State's All-Sports Museum, and to Jackie Esposito and Paul Dzyak in the Penn State Archive department for their gracious assistance with photos. As always, I must thank my wife, Bernice, for her research and editorial help. A guy never had a better teammate.

INTRODUCTION

Around the time Penn State was celebrating the 100th anniversary of its football program, Joe Paterno quipped to reporters: "I haven't been here all that time, it only seems that way."

Paterno might have been kidding, but he wasn't very far from the truth. As the Nittany Lions headed into the 2003 season, Paterno was entering his 54th season at Penn State—38 as a head coach.

Because Paterno has been associated with Penn State football success for so long, it's hard to imagine the Nittany Lions without him. But, believe it or not, there already was a rich football tradition in place when he took over as head coach in 1966.

The Nittany Lions had nationally prominent teams in the 1920s under Hugo Bezdek, playing in the 1923 Rose Bowl. The Bob Higgins era featured an unbeaten season in 1947 and an appearance in the 1948 Cotton Bowl. And Rip Engle lifted the Lions to new levels of national prominence in the 1950s and 1960s, taking Penn State to four bowl games.

Engle made many smart moves during his 16-year tenure at Penn State. One of the smartest was bringing along Paterno as an assistant when he took over as the Nittany Lions' head football coach in 1950. Paterno was an unknown coaching commodity at that point, although he had played for Engle at Brown. As a quarterback, Paterno was hardly the prototype at the position. He can't run and he can't pass, it was said of Paterno the player. All he could do was think—and win!

As a coach, he did the same. And Penn State football was never the same again.

Though Paterno surely must be given the lion's share of credit for raising the profile of Penn State football to unprecedented heights, he is still just a part of the historic puzzle.

He would readily tell you that he learned at the feet of the master, having Rip Engle as his mentor. Engle built on the great foundation of Bob Higgins. And Higgins was the beneficiary of the steps established by Hugo Bezdek.

It all started in 1887 with Penn State's first official football team.

Hopefully, by the time you finish reading these stories, you will have learned something about Penn State's colorful football history. I hope you will find them entertaining as well as informative.

—Ken Rappoport

PREFACE

I n the spring of 1972 I visited Penn State for the first time to research a book on the history of the Nittany Lions football team.

I was a young sports writer with The Associated Press in New York at the time and looking forward to working on my very first book, a lifelong dream. Talk about happiness. Just thinking about it, I would click my heels as I walked to work at the AP building at Rockefeller Center.

John Morris, then the sports information director at Penn State, did all he could to help open doors. He also opened his files, a treasure trove of photographs and newspaper and magazine articles.

That was just the beginning. An interview was arranged with Rip Engle. The former Penn State coach told me a story about a lesson learned from a mule (see Chapter Five). Then came Joe Paterno. He joined me and my wife, Bernice, for lunch at the Nittany Lion Inn. Well, we had lunch. Paterno just ordered black coffee. Then he went through his career and life, telling us among other things about his notable "Grand Experiment" at Penn State.

But perhaps the highlight of the visit was an interview with three old timers from Penn State's storied past—Dutch Herman, Joe Bedenk and Dutch Ricker. We spent an evening with them as they swapped football stories over applesauce cake and coffee.

Herman went back further than the other two, having played quarterback for Penn State in 1909 and 1911. Bedenk was an All-American guard on the 1923 team, a longtime assistant to Bob Higgins and a head coach himself for one year. And Ricker was a guard on the Nittany Lion teams of the late 1920s. From these gentlemen, I learned what football was like in the "good, old days." Well, they weren't always so good for quarterbacks, according to Herman. Let him tell it in his own words (Chapter One).

Before the evening was over, it was no longer evening. Now past midnight, my wife and I had been filled with a large serving of Nittany Lion lore—yet hungry for more.

Herman, Bedenk and Ricker are all gone now. As are Engle and Morris. But I was thrilled that I was able to know these people and record their stories for posterity.

They are all in this book, along with many others I have gathered in interviews and research throughout my sports writing career. There has been a lot more football history to record since the 1970s, as you well know. I hope you find the stories memorable. I know they will always be for me, thanks to one particular evening with three old time football players at Penn State.

—Ken Rappoport

GETTING THE BALL ROLLING
1880s–1899

To start at the beginning: The first college football game in America was played in 1869 between Rutgers and Princeton. Everyone is sure of that.

The same can't be said of Penn State football.

The Nittany Lions played their first season in 1887. Or in 1881, depending on whom you believe.

Although a team in 1881 isn't recognized in the Penn State media guide, it did actually exist for one game. Pay attention to I.P. McCreary, who described himself as a referee of the 1881 contest between Penn State and Bucknell.

"Prior to '77," McCreary once wrote, "there had been some desultory football kicking by the students on the old front campus with no organization. But in the fall of 1880, as football was becoming quite a feature in the other colleges, we at Penn State caught the fever and an organization was perfected."

By the early part of the 1881 school year, McCreary said players had a book of football rules (Peck & Snyders) to study and a game lined up against Bucknell.

"A uniform was decided upon, and old Billy Hoover of Shingletown Gap was secured to make the 'togs,'" McCreary

When Joe Paterno took over the head coaching job at Penn State in 1966, he began a tradition of winning with athletes who were also good students.

recalled. "Strenuous practice was instituted and as I recall it, we left State College on Friday afternoon, November 11, in two conveyances for Spring Mills, at which point we left our rigs at a livery and took a train for Lewisburg." There the Penn State players were "met by the Bucknell boys" and "we were royally entertained by them."

The "Bucknell boys" were most hospitable in all ways. They even handed Penn State the game, 9-0.

Penn State concedes that a contest was played at Bucknell in 1881, but does not list it in the record book. "The nature of the game was considered to be a rugby-style scrimmage," notes the Penn State football media guide, "thus it is not counted as an intercollegiate football game."

The first mention of a football team in the media guide is 1887. The captain was George Linsz, possibly because he owned the only football. In those days Penn State's football team was actually known as the "Nittanymen." Not until 1906 were Penn State's athletic teams called the Nittany Lions.

Everything was in short supply. In fact, Penn State suited up only 12 players for the first official game. There was a good reason for that.

"There were only 12 uniforms available," said Charley Hildebrand, a member of that team.

The Nittanymen went 2-0 that year, both victories over Bucknell. Penn State football was off and running.

Immediately after Penn State's 9-0 win over Bucknell in 1881, I. P. McCreary went straight to the Western Union office. He was going to send a telegram to his friend John W. Stewart at Bellefonte, who could relay the news of Penn State's glorious victory to the waiting students.

McCreary crafted the message: "We have met the enemy and they are ours; nine to nothing!"

He handed the piece of paper to the Western Union clerk. But the operator at Lewisburg, for some reason or other, was reluctant to send the message. Perhaps he was upset that Penn State had beaten his beloved Bucknell team.

"You send it, or I'll come over the counter and send it myself," said the excitable McCreary.

The operator sent it.

A Zero Contribution

Sam Boyle's one season in 1899 as coach at Penn State had its ups and downs—mostly downs as his 4-6-1 record would attest.

However, Boyle did manage a few impressive accomplishments that season.

His Penn State team beat Army 6-0 in its first meeting with the Cadets. It would be 60 years before Penn State would win again at West Point.

Under Boyle, Penn State held five opponents scoreless. And when he left State College to coach at Dickinson the following season, he showed he had not lost his shutout touch. Ironically, one of the teams he shut out was Penn State.

Really, It Could Have Been Worse

The score was 106-0, with Penn State on the short end. Really. The licking at Lehigh in 1889 wasn't exactly a high point in Nittany Lion football.

Dutch Herman, who later played quarterback for Penn State, recounted a story of the worst football defeat in Penn State history.

"There were no telegraph, no wire services, nothing of that type to find out how the game came out," Herman said in a 1972 interview. "In those days, the students would meet the players at the train station when they came back. The students were very enthusiastic and several thousand went down to meet the returning players."

Some called for the captain to come out and tell the crowd what had happened. Meanwhile, the score had leaked to the crowd somehow. Although Penn State had lost badly, the captain tried to put a positive spin on things.

"Oh, it was a tough game," he said according to Herman. "It was a good game, though. We played well and did all right."

Then someone in the crowd said, "If you did all right, how did you manage to get beat 106-0?"

Realizing he had been caught in a slight misinterpretation, the captain answered, "Well, we couldn't get at the son-of-a-gun who had the ball!"

Actually Penn State did have an excuse. Due to injuries suffered in a 26-0 loss to Lafayette two days earlier, Penn State could only field a team of nine instead of the usual eleven.

The Lehigh game was halted with five minutes remaining, otherwise the score could have been more lopsided.

Not So Pretty in Pink

A football team in pink? Don't laugh.

Back in the 1880s when Penn State was starting to play football, players wanted something "bright and attractive" for their uniforms, according to George Meek, Class of 1890.

"We could not use red or orange, as these colors were already in use by other colleges," Meek said. "So we had a very deep pink—really cerise—which with black made a very pretty combination."

Meek had striped pink and black uniform jerseys made up, and the color scheme was greeted with an enthusiastic response from students. Until a couple of weeks' exposure to the sun. The cerise started to fade quickly and soon the uniforms were white and black.

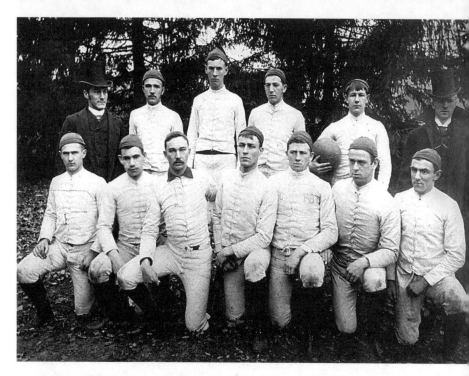

The first official football team at Penn State in 1887. There is evidence that football was played at State College as early as 1881.

"So the colors were quickly changed to blue and white," said Meek.

Thus the dawn of Penn State's long-standing school colors.

Clothes Make the Team

Penn State had no coach in its first official football season of 1887. It only had one football, owned by George Linsz. And it only played two games.

If nothing else, the team was stylish. The Penn State boys were attired in tight-fitting canvas jackets and knee-length pants. There was virtually no padding.

The front of the uniform bore the initials "PSC-FB" (Penn State College Football). Literally topping off things, the Penn Staters wore snug "beanies" on top of their heads.

Hats off to Penn State! The "Nittanymen" beat Bucknell twice, by scores of 54-0 and 24-0.

Twenty Bucks Is Twenty Bucks

Today 20 dollars won't get you too far. In the 1880s, it was actually the amount of money that Penn State earned as a visiting team for a game. Along with meals.

That was the guarantee that Penn State was promised for a game at Lewisburg, Pennsylvania, on Oct. 27, 1888 against Bucknell.

Unfortuately for both teams, the game ended in a dispute and no score was recorded

Penn State still got to eat free and keep the 20, however.

Football, by George

Imagine playing for Penn State for four years, then switching allegiances to play for rival Pitt? It sounds crazy, but in the 1890s it was par for the course under the loose eligibility requirements of the day.

So meet George Hoskins, who doubled as trainer and player at Penn State from 1892-95. The same George Hoskins who switched over to Pitt in 1896 and instantly became the "enemy" for more reasons than one.

Hoskins was Penn State's first director of physical training and first instructor of physical education in 1892. Hoskins was an innovator. He organized the first spring practices at State College and turned out compelling teams (a 17-4-4 record in four seasons). Hoskins also played center and was looked up to as a role model on and off the field.

Hoskins's arrival signaled a forward movement in the Penn State football program. Newly named Beaver Field was being fitted for a 500-seat grandstand, complete with projecting blue-and-white roof and three flagpoles.

When Penn State first played Pitt (then Western University of Pittsburgh) in 1893, the game was a model of sportsmanship.

"We must compliment the players on the marked absence of slugging," wrote the Penn State newspaper, *Free Lance,* following Penn State's 32-0 victory. "Both teams behaved like gentlemen. We want the Western boys to come again and come often."

Three years later, Hoskins had joined Pitt and now the atmosphere was a little different when the teams played. Now playing center for the Panthers, Hoskins instigated one of the biggest football brawls ever seen at State College. Penn State won 10-4, but that wasn't the story of the day.

Wrote the *Free Lance:* "The second game of the season on Beaver Field with Western University of Pittsburgh did more injury to the prestige of the game of football than its promoter can repair in many years." The newspaper particularly singled out Hoskins for "an exhibition of the unmanly defiance of all fair rules which degrades the game."

One little brawl and how soon they forget.

Seven Teams Out

George Hoskins's Penn State teams were known for their strong defenses. From 1892-95 under Hoskins, Penn State recorded 15 shutouts in 25 games and allowed just six points in each of four other games.

The 1894 squad, captained by Benjamin Fisher, might have been Hoskins's strongest. On the way to a 6-0-1 record, Penn State outscored opponents 179-18.

Penn State put fear into other teams, for sure. After Penn State humbled Lafayette 72-0 in the second game, perhaps it was no accident—even though schedules were disrupted in wholesale quantity in those days — that seven opponents canceled games with the awesome "Nittanymen."

HOLLENBACK, HARLOW AND A GOLDEN ERA
1900–1917

The early part of the 20th century featured a series of momentous breakthroughs: the first long-distance radio transmission by Marconi, the initial flight of the Wright Brothers and the introduction of the Model-T and the assembly line by Ford. Not to mention the first World Series and Robert Peary claiming the North Pole in an early version of the moon landing.

At Penn State, the football team made breakthroughs as well thanks to W. N. "Pop" Golden. Hired as a physical trainer, Golden stuck around for a dozen years in the capacities of coach, athletic director and recruiter and helped to raise the football program, and Penn State sports in general, to new levels.

The highlight football years during this time were 1911 and 1912, when teams coached by Bill Hollenback went unbeaten in 17 games. The Lions extended that streak to 19 in 1913. The 1912 squad, lead by quarterback Eugene "Shorty" Miller and fullback Pete Mauthe, was recognized as one of Penn State's great early teams. Penn State shut out its first two opponents. When the Nittany Lions gave up six points to

Cornell in the third game, they decided enough was enough. So they simply blanked the rest of their opponents that season to finish with seven shutouts in eight games.

Other coaches who led the Nittany Lions from 1900-17: Dan Reed, Tom Fennell, Jack Hollenback and Dick Harlow.

First Class Seat

Many football coaches are superstitious. Dick Harlow might have carried it to new levels.

Harlow had coached some fine Penn State teams from 1915-17. He continued his successful career at Colgate, Western Maryland and Harvard, winning a coach of the year award in 1936 while with the Crimson.

At Western Maryland, Harlow had an abundance of good players, not to mention an abundance of superstitions. One was the seating arrangement on the team bus to Baltimore, where Western Maryland played its home games.

It could be a trial for the players—one particular player—as Rip Engle once remembered.

"Poor Pete Gumsack broke his collarbone in the third game of his senior year and he was out for the rest of the season," said Engle, who played for Harlow at Western Maryland long before his brilliant Penn State coaching days. "No matter—he had to ride that bus to Baltimore and sit in the same seat for the year, arm in sling and all."

Harlow's little eccentricity obviously didn't hurt. Western Maryland finished the 1929 season with an 11-0 record.

He Had It All the Way

When Bill Hollenback was coaching at Penn State, he wasn't hard to miss. According to one national magazine,

Hollenback "was an excitable creature and created a great deal of havoc by cruising up and down the sidelines during the game."

When Hollenback was hired by Penn State in 1909 at the age of 23, he was the youngest head football coach in the country. He proceeded to lead the Nittany Lions to a 5-0-2 season, their first unbeaten year since 1894. He left for one season and came back to coach from 1911-14, leading the Nittany Lions to two more unbeaten seasons and a 19-game unbeaten streak.

One day Penn State was facing Pitt when Hollenback was doing his frantic thing, "cruising" up and down the sidelines. Suddenly, he came to a dead halt when he heard halfback Pete Mauthe calling for a place kick from 58 yards.

What, was he crazy? Hollenback called to his assistant Dick Harlow to find another halfback to replace Mauthe. Harlow, not much older than the players and just as animated as Hollenback, started at one end of the bench trying to find a player to substitute for Mauthe.

"He overturned water buckets, mangled third-string quarterbacks and half fell, half careened his way along the sidelines," the magazine reported.

But before Harlow could find a sub, Mauthe had kicked the ball clear through the uprights. When Harlow finally got back to Hollenback with a replacement, the head coach was wreathed in smiles.

"A great play!" Hollenback exclaimed. "Exactly the signal I had in mind."

Talk About Tough

When he played at Penn State from 1910-11, Dick Harlow developed a reputation as one of the toughest tackles around. His specialty was blocking punts, and he was one of the top players in the country in this category.

It stood to reason he would be just as tough as a coach, and he was. At Penn State from 1915-17, Harlow drove his players unmercifully in practice.

According to one national magazine, this exchange occurred between a player and his friends after he had just hobbled back to his quarters after a session under Harlow:

"Do you know what we had today? We had blocking—live blocking. We dumped each other all over the field."

"Great heavens," cried the player's friends. "And what will you be doing tomorrow?"

"Tomorrow," said the player, "we start in with the hand grenades."

Give Him a Break

Where do you draw the line between heroism and stupidity? For Dick Harlow, it was admittedly more of the latter than the former at one particular moment of his Penn State football career.

He had broken a bone in his ankle and ordinarily would have gone to the hospital. Instead, the big game with Pitt was coming up and he desperately wanted to play.

"We made an issue of it," Harlow said. "Either I played or we'd all be mad. Pete Mauthe, the captain, demanded that I have my rights and (coach Bill) Hollenback gave in."

The trainer made a plaster cast for Harlow's leg and wrapped it around iron splints.

"I came to the field on crutches and got rid of them in the field house," Harlow said.

Then Harlow went out to his tackle position and—amazingly—played the whole 60 minutes. After the game he went back to crutches. He had to stay on them for six weeks.

"It wasn't bravery—it was dumbness," Harlow later concluded. "I learned something from it at that. I learned that a player half as good is twice as good as a man out there with a broken leg."

Lionized

When Dick Harlow agreed to coach the Harvard football team in 1935, there were some eyebrows raised at Cambridge.

There were concerns about Harlow, even though he had turned out good football teams at Penn State, Colgate and Western Maryland. A troubling legend persisted throughout his coaching career. And the story took on a life of its own, growing with time. When Harlow left Penn State, as the story goes, the entire football team walked out and followed him to Colgate. Needless to say, it caused an uproar.

Outrageous as that might have seemed, Harvard athletic director Bill Bingham was obligated to check out the story. After some investigation, Bingham concluded in faultless Ivy League logic that no such thing would happen when Harlow moved to Harvard.

"I don't imagine anybody who knows Harvard entrance requirements will be worried by an influx of halfbacks who can run better than they can read," Bingham said.

That did not stop Harlow from hiring some former Penn Staters as assistant coaches, however. Neil Stabley was brought in to coach the freshmen and Mike Palm to coach the backfield and place kickers.

Thrown for a Gain

It was before the turn of the 20th century, the "good, old days" of college football. Well, not so good for the quarterback.

"He'd have these large loops on his belt and a teammate on each side of him would hoist him up and throw him over the line," Dutch Herman once recalled.

"They gained ground, but lost a lot of quarterbacks that way."

Herman played quarterback for Penn State in 1909 and 1911. Luckily for him, the barbaric nonsense of quarterback tossing had been abolished by then. Actually, the early 1900s saw many other changes in football rules to eliminate unnecessary violence.

"They thought it would be a better idea if they threw the ball instead of the quarterback," said Herman, recounting the early days of Nittany Lion football in a 1972 interview.

Quarterbacks everywhere had to be relieved.

What's in a Nickname?

He was nicknamed "Mother" but hit more like your big brother. In 1906 William T. "Mother" Dunn anchored one of Penn State's great defensive teams of the early 1900s.

Amazingly, that season Penn State shut out nine opponents in 10 games, allowing only 10 points in all. Dunn was a key defensive player at roving center and became Penn State's first All-American. According to one writer, Dunn was "a powerful charger on offense—a terror to opponents on defense" in those days of two-way play.

Dunn didn't let injuries keep him on the sidelines. He once played with a broken collarbone against Navy. Another time he discarded crutches against the advice of his coach to play a career-ending game against Pitt. And he had one of his biggest days against Harvard despite wearing a steel brace on an injured knee.

Remembered onetime Penn State coach Rip Engle: "The Harvard boys, knowing that Mother had an injury, tried to go for the knee as soon as play started. Instead, the big Harvard center received full treatment from the brace and was taken from the game. The substitute steered clear of Mother's injured knee."

Oddly, Dunn had never played football before he came to Penn State. He had read somewhere about the "flying tackle," though, and used it to good advantage in his first day of practice at State College. Dunn so impressed everybody that he was immediately made a starter.

And the nickname?

It occurred during Dunn's freshman year. As the freshman class president, he was leading his classmates across campus when a sophomore student blared out:

"There goes Mother Dunn and all her baby chicks."

The nickname stuck.

Quickly Reversing His Field

Bill Hollenback's coaching career at Penn State was short but sweet—five seasons, interrupted by a year at Missouri, and 41 games in all.

Without question, his 1912 team stood as one of the early giants of Penn State football. That season the Lions went 8-0 with seven shutouts, outscoring their opponents 285-6.

Not that Hollenback was always on the same page with his players. But he was quick to give them their due whenever they deserved it.

Like in the game against Pitt. Penn State was leading the Panthers 31-0 in the fourth quarter. The Lions had the ball on their own 20 and lined up in a kick formation.

No, wait. Quarterback Shorty Miller diagnosed a perfect opportunity for an end run. With Hollenback watching intently from the sidelines, his team changed into another formation.

Not so fast. Suddenly, Miller switched signals again. Now he called for a pass over the middle.

Hollenback was frantic. In those days a pass from your own 20 was considered a crime. The hot-tempered coach threw up his hands in dismay, turned to the spectators and shouted:

"Give me a gun! Oh, give me a gun so I can shoot him! He's trying to hand them a touchdown on a platter!"

Too late. By the time Hollenback had finished ranting and raving, the pass had already been made—and completed to Dexter Very. The Penn State receiver raced 70 yards before he was brought down on the Pitt 10.

Hollenback watched the play to its completion, and turned to his bench with a big grin. Without batting an eyelash, he remarked:

"There, by gosh! That's brains and how to use 'em!"

Just like that, Hollenback had gone from wanting to kill a player to complimenting him.

Shorty Miller outracing the field for a loose ball. He quarterbacked one of Penn State's great early teams in 1912.

A Different Kind of Hero

Rip Engle was passing through Hawaii on his way back from a coaching clinic in Japan in 1954 when he stopped to visit a friend. It was none other than Mother Dunn, Penn State's first All-American in 1906.

While at Penn State, Dunn had never sought the limelight, remarking many times, "I don't want any darn publicity." Things hadn't changed when Engle caught up with him many years later. Dunn had become a virtual recluse, working as a plantation doctor on the island of Maui.

The onetime sports hero was now a hero of a different sort to the island folk. Now he was battling diseases rather than football opponents. And, as expected, Dunn was extremely conscientious. He never drank because he was his community's only physician. He once lost a finger because he refused to wear protective gloves while working with patients under X-Ray equipment. He felt that he could work better without the gloves.

Dunn made a rare trip to the main island to see Engle. The Penn State football coach was glad he did. After spending four hours with Dunn, Engle came away thinking, "This is a night I'll remember all my life."

One of the things Dunn said that stuck in Engle's mind:

"One thing boys in football ought to remember is that if you play dirty, you get it right back with interest. If you do it against a weaker man, you are only hurting yourself."

After the chat, Engle remarked of the remarkable Dunn: "He's still an All-American in my book."

Dunn died on November 19, 1962 in Hawaii after many years of service to his community, a true All-American to his fellow islanders.

Uh, His Mistake

It was before the 1912 season and coach Bill Hollenback had high hopes for Penn State's football prospects. Not so for one particular graduate, who had returned to help teach Penn State players some fundamentals.

"The backfield is good," the graduate said in assessing the team, "but the line is weak."

The linemen took umbrage, and Hollenback decided to give the visitor a chance to back up his statement. He put the ball on the five-yard line and gave the former player five tries to put it over. After the third try, he was back on the 20-yard line and much the worse for wear.

"He decided that he had had enough and that his judgment was a little off," recalled a Penn State tackle by the name of "Dad" Engle.

Oh, boy, was it. That season Penn State's defense shut out seven opponents and allowed a total of merely six points in eight games. It was one of the greatest defensive performances in Penn State football history.

Goodbye, Columbus

When Penn State visited Ohio State in 1912, there was no love lost between the teams. Despite running roughshod over their first six opponents, the Nittany Lions were underdogs to the Buckeyes. If you believed the local newspapers, that is. All of them predicted an easy Buckeye win.

When they played the game, it was a different story. Penn State rushed to a big early lead. It was too much for the Buckeye players, who were throwing punches and needling the Nittany Lions. Penn State's Al Wilson, for one, had to be removed from the game when some teeth were removed from his mouth by an Ohio State sucker punch.

An Ohio State tackle by the name of Barraklow had been challenging Penn State quarterback Shorty Miller throughout the game. Finally, Miller decided to show him a little humility. According to Wilson, this was the conversation on the field:

"Run one through me," Barraklow said.

"Right-o," said Miller, then turned to fullback Pete Mauthe. "Mr. Mauthe, will you kindly escort the ball through Mr. Barraklow's position."

"Check," said Mauthe and ran eight yards for a first down.

The Buckeyes simply weren't the same after that. The game soon dissolved into a massive brawl involving spectators. The game was halted with nine minutes to go, and Penn State left Columbus with a 37-0 victory.

A Matter of Pride

Many a college football team that prides itself on defense likes nothing better than to hold an opponent scoreless. Imagine doing it for an entire season.

The 1912 Penn State team came close. The only opponent to cross the Nittany Lions' goal line that season was Cornell. After shutting out Carnegie Tech and Washington & Jefferson, the Nittany Lions gave up a touchdown to the Big Red on an intercepted pass.

As the teams lined up for Cornell's extra-point try, Penn State end Al Wilson recalled the reaction of teammate "Dad" Engle, one of the Lions' tackles.

"Engle, who never cussed and was rather quiet normally, broke out with the greatest array of cuss words you ever heard. He ended with, 'I'll be damned if I'll ever stand under another goal post like this.'"

The varsity never did, finishing the season with shutouts over Gettysburg, Penn, Villanova, Ohio State and Pitt.

Showing Them the Money

Back in the days when it was OK for coaches to loan money to athletes, Dick Harlow did his share. Probably more than his share.

Harlow, a former Penn State player who also coached at Penn State as well as Colgate, Western Maryland and Harvard, once figured he had coached over 600 players. He always was generous with his time and money.

When he retired in 1947, Harlow went over his records and totaled the amount of money he had loaned to players over the years "for books, illness, trouble at home or even to go home for the holiday."

The figure amounted to about $27,000—a lot of money now and certainly worth even more then.

Guess what? Those were also the days when athletes actually paid back their loans. Only one loan of $165 was outstanding. And there was a good reason for that, as Harlow once remembered:

"The boy was killed in World War II."

Two for the Money

It was 1915, long before Bob Higgins became the legendary and revered Penn State football coach known as the "Hig." At the time, he was still a sophomore with his best football years ahead of him.

This story concerns the time Higgins had to duplicate a touchdown catch after a penalty, which usually only happens in movies.

Penn State and Lehigh were scoreless with time running out in the first half when Higgins caught a pass from Stan Ewing and raced 15 yards into the end zone.

Touchdown Penn State! But hold on—the Nittany Lions had 12 men on the field instead of the regulation 11. A substitute, sent in by coach Dick Harlow with instructions, had wandered onto the field too soon.

When the substitute, Chuck Yerger, arrived in the huddle, he was greeted by a pretty angry bunch of teammates.

"Coach Harlow says to throw that pass," said Yerger, a pained expression on his face.

"We just did!" chorused his Penn State teammates.

The Nittany Lions quickly went into their formation. They called the same play. Ewing threw the ball to Higgins in the same spot and he scored in a virtual replica of the first TD play.

This one counted, and Penn State had a 7-0 victory.

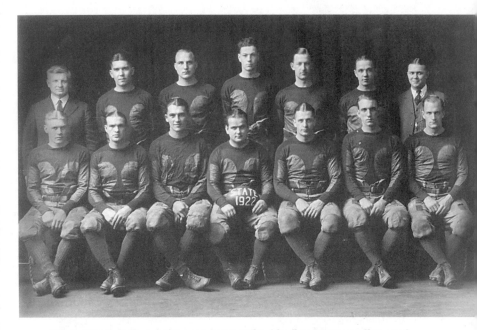

Hugo Bezdek (top left) was known for his fiery personality, and he brought almost instant success to the Penn State Football program during his tenure as head coach (1918-1929).

BEZDEK'S BOYS
1918–1929

It was the "Golden Age" of sports with such personalities as Babe Ruth, Red Grange and the Four Horsemen stealing the headlines. These were sports' first superstars. There was also Knute Rockne, who propelled Notre Dame to the forefront and raised the consciousness of college football with his inspirational salesmanship.

Penn State football had its own golden age, thanks to a compelling coach by the name of Hugo Bezdek. With his tough training methods, he brought almost instant success to the Penn State football program in the aftermath of the First World War.

Those fine postwar teams featured All-Americans Bob Higgins, Charley Way, Glenn Killinger and Joe Bedenk. The Nittany Lions were invited to the Rose Bowl, their first bowl game, at the end of the 1922 season. It was an era of unprecedented success at State College. At one point from 1919-22, the Lions put together a 30-game unbeaten streak.

Bezdek, who also doubled as athletic director, remained in that position after his coaching days were over at Penn State. Simultaneously pictured as a savior and a dictator, Bezdek was usually controversial but never dull.

"He would be the first to tell you he was not running a popularity contest," said Harry "Lighthorse" Wilson, who played under Bezdek in the early 1920s. "He was tough, but he put out and demanded that others put out, too. He taught good football and he insured that you were in condition to play 60 minutes."

Ditching It

Hugo Bezdek was a coach highly respected but wholly feared by his players at Penn State.

As the story goes, Bezdek was driving some of his players to a game. While making a turn, Bezdek's car edged dangerously close to a ditch.

None of the players dared say anything to their authoritarian coach for fear of provoking his wrath.

"You tell him," one whispered in the back seat.

"No, you," said another, quietly.

By the time anyone built up the courage to speak, the car had rolled into the ditch. Fortunately, no one was hurt. But Bezdek and his players had to walk to the game that day.

Getting a Leg Up

As a football coach, Hugo Bezdek was as tough as they come, often responding to a player's injured leg with the suggestion that he "cut it off."

Once Bezdek was involved in a foot race with one of his players when he injured his own leg and had to be carted off the field.

At which time a voice, protected by darkness, bellowed to Bezdek: "Cut it off."

Naturally, none of the players admitted to making the remark.

Those Are the Breaks

Hugo Bezdek's "Bloody Tuesday" practices were legendary during his time as coach at Penn State from 1918-29. Players were lucky to get through the practices, no less games, without injury.

One player recalled, "We'd scrimmage every defense in the world until everybody couldn't stand up anymore."

Joe Bedenk, an All-America guard on the 1923 team under Bezdek and later an assistant to coach Bob Higgins, broke his collarbone while tackling dummies during one practice session.

Bezdek ordered Bedenk to take "21 laps around the track." The coach reasoned that there was nothing wrong with Bedenk's legs even if his collarbone was broken.

"I ran 21 laps around that damn track," Bedenk recalled.

And, of course, three days later he suited up for the game, broken collarbone and all.

It's Something the Coach Should Know

Since joining the Big Ten in 1993, Penn State's football games with Ohio State, Michigan and the like have taken on a whole new meaning.

It could be many years, though, before the Nittany Lions ever develop a rivalry to match the one with Pitt. From 1893-2000, the Lions and Panthers clashed 96 times with Penn State leading the series, 50-42-4.

After nearly 100 years of banging heads with Pitt, it should come as no surprise that some of the most storied moments in Nittany Lions history occurred in this fierce and bitter rivalry. The longest touchdown pass ever thrown by a Penn State player, for instance.

Early in the 1919 Thanksgiving Day game, the Nittany Lions pulled off a play that "will be seen perhaps once in a hundred collegiate football games," according to one newspaper account.

With the ball backed up against the Penn State goal line, the Nittany Lions went into a kick formation. Instead of kicking, though, fullback Harold Hess tossed a short screen pass to Bob Higgins. Penn State's All-America end did the rest, romping 92 yards for the longest pass-and-run play in Nittany Lions history. It started the Lions to a 20-0 victory.

It was a totally unexpected play, even more so because Hess was taking the snap. He had never thrown a pass for Penn State and never would again.

Although Hugo Bezdek was the Penn State coach at the time, he couldn't claim credit for the play. That went to assistant Dick Harlow, who had been scouting the Panthers for weeks. Harlow had noticed that whenever the Panthers had an opponent with its backs against the goal line, they usually rushed nine or ten men.

The Nittany Lions practiced the fake kick play in the week leading up the game. For some reason or other, they forgot to tell Bezdek about it until the last minute. When they finally did, he was naturally upset.

"It sounds OK," he said with a growl. "But next time let me know what's going on around here."

That Fighting Spirit

Before Hugo Bezdek came to Penn State to coach football in 1918, his reputation preceded him. Stories about his rough-and-ready style had already made him a controversial figure. His legendary temper came into play when he once battled a baseball pitcher on a train from Pittsburgh to New York. When they got off, he and the Brooklyn Dodgers' Burleigh Grimes shook hands, so the story goes.

Bezdek added another story to his quick-fisted legend when he took Penn State to the 1923 Rose Bowl.

When the Nittany Lions arrived late for their clash with Southern Cal, Trojans coach Elmer Henderson was blazing mad. He accused Bezdek of delaying the start of the game so that temperatures could cool off a bit for the cold-weather Lions.

The coaches got into a violent argument at midfield, while some 43,000 fans cooled their heels, waiting impatiently for the game to begin. All the while, Bezdek maintained that his team was held up in the Rose Bowl parade traffic jam. The Penn State coach had to be dragged away before he took a swing at Henderson.

The Nittany Lions, however, didn't put up much of a fight themselves. In their first-ever visit to a bowl game, they lost to the Trojans, 14-3.

Frequent Flyer Club

These days, all roads lead to Penn State—literally and figuratively. The Nittany Lions have become one of the centers of the college football universe.

That wasn't necessarily the case in the 1920s when Penn State was trying to make a name for itself on a national scale and trying to find national powers to visit them. State College was not the most accessible place in the world.

As Robert Maxwell, sports editor of the *Philadelphia Public Ledger*, wrote, "State College is located in Center County and Center County can be located by means of a large map, a compass and an experienced guide."

So it was then that Penn State traveled far and wide to meet "name" teams, playing Washington in Seattle; Harvard in Cambridge, Massachusetts; Syracuse in the Polo Grounds in New York; Georgia Tech and West Virginia in Yankee Stadium in New York, and Navy in Washington, D.C., and Philadelphia.

The road-heavy schedule didn't seem to bother the Lions. In 1921, they traveled 8,500 miles while playing half their 10-game schedule on the road. Yet Penn State's road warriors managed to go through the year unbeaten at 8-0-2 under Hugo Bezdek.

It was the start of great things during Bezdek's coaching reign at State College.

In So Many Words

The 1921 season featured a string of smashing victories for the undefeated Penn State football team. The most dramatic game of the year, however, was one that ended in neither victory nor defeat.

Not many games live up to their advance billing, but the one between Eastern powers Penn State and Harvard did that year.

The Crimson stormed to an early 14-0 lead, only to see Penn State quarterback Glenn Killinger guide the Nittany Lions to three straight scores.

Then after Harvard tied the game at 21 in the late going, Killinger again drove the Nittany Lions to the shadow of the Crimson's goal posts in the gathering dusk.

The stadium, of course, was without lights at the time. Joe Bedenk, the Penn State guard, recalled that the fans' cigarettes in the near dark looked like "fireflies" scattered around Harvard's stadium.

Penn State's last drive fell short as Harvard's defense stiffened and the teams walked away with a hard-fought 21-21 tie. It inspired this long and florid lead from one Philadelphia sports writer, apparently doing his best to imitate Grantland Rice:

"In an October gloaming whose gathering gloom covered the vast stadium with a fleecy veil of dusk, Harvard, her

Crimson back plastered squarely against the wall and trembling on the threshold of her first defeat in five years, awakened and quickened into a fury like a tigress robbed of her cubs today, drove back Penn State's magnificent warriors with a savage attack and scored a touchdown that evened a 21 to 21 contest in a game as spectacular as any gridiron has known in the past 20 years."

In short, a whale of a game.

Harried

The great 1921 Penn State-Harvard game always held vivid memories for Nittany Lions halfback Harry "Lighthorse" Wilson—not all of them pleasant. As Wilson told in a 1970s interview:

"Someone kicked out one of my front teeth. I tried to call time out, but someone said, 'What for? We can't stop for a little thing like that!' So we didn't. Later that night at the railroad station in Boston, the referee came up to me and said, 'Here, Wilson, here is that tooth you were looking for this afternoon.'"

It was before that game, as Wilson recalled, that the Penn State coaching staff warned the players "that the Harvard boys would steal the ball from you at every opportunity."

Shortly after getting into the game, Wilson broke through for a 60-yard run that ended near Harvard's five-yard line.

"It seemed like the whole Harvard team fell on me at once," Wilson remembered. "Remembering the warnings, I shut my eyes and clung onto the ball with both arms. Sure enough, there seemed to be a dozen hands tugging at it and it felt like they were never going to stop.

"Finally, I heard [Penn State quarterback] Glenn Killinger's voice saying, 'Come on, Harry, give the referee the ball.'"

Jekyll and Herman

He was a dignified professor of history. Until he put on his coaching hat, that is. Then Dutch Herman changed personalities.

"He was a good coach and quite a character," Harry "Lighthorse" Wilson once recalled of Herman, who coached freshman football, varsity basketball and scouted opponents for the varsity football team. Wilson, an All-American halfback for the Penn State football team, also played some basketball under Herman. He remembered one night when the Nittany Lions were doing poorly.

"Dutch left the bench, went up to the stands and started booing us from the bleachers."

It wasn't exactly a surprise for Penn State athletes. In football, they had seen Herman's act before.

"If things were going wrong on the football field he would relieve his feelings by yelling, spitting and tearing his hat from front to rear on his head—the hat he saved especially for games."

Herman was a stickler for rules. For one thing, he didn't like his players to smoke. Wilson remembered:

"I was walking across campus sneaking a few puffs on a cigarette when I ran into Dutch. I quickly stuck my hand and cigarette into my coat pocket! Well, he stopped and talked and talked until the lining of my pocket was well burned out. While he never said anything about the cigarettes, I am sure he knew exactly what he was doing, as well what I had been doing."

No Horsing Around

Harry "Lighthorse" Wilson had the unique distinction of being named an All-American for two different college teams —Penn State and Army. When the great halfback played at Penn State from 1921-23, he was selected by a group called the "500 Coaches and Percy Haughton," the legendary Harvard coach. When Wilson transferred to Army, he was named an All-American by a group consisting of three other high-profile coaches—Knute Rockne, Pop Warner and Tad Jones.

Good as he was, though, Wilson had a hard time breaking into the Penn State lineup at first.

"I was a substitute who just went along for the ride whenever we had road games," Wilson once recalled of his first year on the Penn State varsity. Wilson's first taste of action, in fact, came halfway through the 1921 season in the Harvard game.

"They had scored twice real quick and [coach Hugo] Bezdek didn't look too happy about it," Wilson recalled. "We subs were sitting in open bleachers at the time, and Bezdek turned to me and growled, 'Wilson, warm up.' I got a little nervous. I got up and ran around and ran around until I got pooped. I was so tired I had to sit down and rest. And just as I sat down, Bezdek screamed, 'Where's Wilson?'"

It didn't take Bezdek long to find out. Before long, Wilson broke off a long run that helped the Nittany Lions rally to tie a great Harvard team, 21-21.

"I managed to run 60 yards or so shortly after I got in," Wilson said. "I don't know how."

He Just Killed 'Em

Glenn Killinger never made the same mistake twice, or so it seemed. When he did make a mistake, he made sure the other team paid for it.

Witness his performance in Penn State's 1921 game with Georgia Tech at the Polo Grounds in New York.

"They kicked off and the ball went to Killinger," Wilson once recalled. "He fumbled and they recovered on the 20-yard line and went in for a touchdown."

On the next kickoff, Georgia Tech once again sent the ball Killinger's way.

"This time, he grabbed it and ran it back for a touchdown. They were never the same again. We beat 'em good."

Final score: Penn State 28, Georgia Tech 7.

One-Man Gang

For an All-American, Harry Wilson never tried to draw too much attention to himself. Except on this particular afternoon in 1923, he simply couldn't help it.

Playing against Navy, Wilson had leaped high into the air to intercept a pass and returned it 50 yards for a touchdown. A little while later, Wilson returned a kickoff 95 yards for another touchdown.

When the Nittany Lions gathered to kick off to Navy after Wilson's second TD, captain Joe Bedenk rallied the team around him. "Come on, gang," he shouted, "let's get started. We haven't done a thing yet; none of us has done a thing except Harry Wilson."

At that moment, a quiet voice was heard from the edge of the huddle. It was Wilson. "*I* haven't done anything. Come on, let's go."

Later in the game, Wilson broke off tackle on a fake reverse play, took off down the sidelines and went 70 yards for yet another score. The final was 21-3 in favor of Penn State, and the halfback who hadn't done anything for his team had scored all their touchdowns.

Bucking the Trend

Beating Bucknell became a habit for Penn State in the early years of their rivalry. But there was a point in the 1920s when the Bisons finally turned things around. They needed a special favor from Penn State's players to do it.

The Nittany Lions had won their first two games of the 1927 season when they took on Bucknell at Beaver Stadium. The Bisons were hurting—particularly fullback Walter Diehl, the team's captain. He was sidelined by a broken ankle.

Even so, the Bisons managed to take a 7-0 lead. The game was tied 7-7 at the half. At that point, Diehl decided that his services were needed, broken ankle or not. Reported The Associated Press: "Captain Diehl was sent in to encourage the team."

The Penn State players, of course, realized that they could knock Diehl out of the game simply by going for his ankle. But when Diehl was dropped for the first time, the Penn State tackler said: "Don't worry, Wally, we'll be careful of your bad ankle."

And each time Penn State tacklers brought Diehl down, they actually went out of their way not to hurt his ankle.

Inspired by Diehl's presence, Bucknell beat Penn State 13-7 to start a six-game winning streak in the series. But the Nittany Lions in that game provided a different kind of inspiration to football in general.

"Whether or not Penn State's fine sportsmanship cost them the victory is hard to say," said a spokesman for Bucknell.

"But if it did, the loss was not commensurable with the gift it made to American football."

Winning and Losing

ESPN would have loved it. Unfortunately, public television did not exist in 1929 or this one would have surely made "Plays of the Week." Talk about exciting endings. Penn State literally pulled one out of the air against Lafayette, thanks to one sensational play after time had run out.

Holding a 3-0 lead with just one second left, the Maroons got set to punt. The ball was in the air when the final whistle blew.

Cooper French, the Penn State safety, caught the ball at his team's 40-yard line with three Lafayette tacklers bearing down on him. Game over, right?

Not quite. French tossed a lateral pass to Frank Diedrich, who raced 60 yards for the winning touchdown. Final: Penn State 6, Lafayette 3.

A near-riot ensued as fans at Beaver Stadium swarmed around in wild celebration. Students carried French and Diedrich off the field on their shoulders.

"The play left some 15,000 persons dumfounded," reported one newspaper.

And one cheerleader without a jacket.

Testifying to the wild celebration, this advertisement signed by varsity cheerleader Izzy Heicklen later appeared in Penn State's student newspaper, *The Collegian*:

"LOST—Cheerleader's jacket at game Saturday. Return to Athletic Association office."

There was no word whether Izzy ever got the jacket back, but he had to be happy with the outcome of the game.

Uncertain Times

The mid- to late 1920s were a time of disillusion in Penn State football. Once-popular Hugo Bezdek had come under fire for a drop off in performance, most notably an inability to beat intrastate rival Pitt. Years removed from the Rose Bowl and 30-game unbeaten streak, Bezdek was finally booted upstairs to the athletic director's office after the 1929 season.

The fault wasn't all Bezdek's. Penn State had wholly endorsed a controversial report by the Carnegie Foundation to de-emphasize football, abolishing athletic scholarships in 1927. The Penn State "purity" campaign plunged the Nittany Lions into their darkest period of history.

So much so that it would take Bob Higgins, Bezdek's replacement, eight years before Penn State had a winning season again.

No Plain Vanilla

With the changing fortunes of Penn State football in the latter part of the 1920s came a change in uniforms.

One season, the Nittany Lions appeared in cardinal. The following season they came out in a blue and white variation using a white stripe running around the chest and white shoulder coverings on a blue background.

The year after, Penn State's players wore a white uniform with blue numbers on the front and back. Finally they returned to the traditional blue shirt at home.

If they did not win too many games, at least the Nittany Lions could say they were colorful.

Room and Bored

The food was good, the sleeping quarters nothing special. It was called the Old Track House, a home away from home for Penn State's football players. There they could eat, sleep and think football.

"All the boys with athletic scholarships lived there," said Harry "Lighthorse" Wilson, who played in the 1920s. "The training table was excellent—the bare barrack-like rooms and furniture and beds left much to be desired."

Wilson recalled there were no hijinks in his time there, either. There was a good reason for it.

"Good conduct was observed mainly because [freshman football coach] Dutch Herman—still a bachelor at the time—slept in the visiting team's quarters on the first floor."

The Right Way

Here comes Charlie Way—there goes Charlie Way.

That just about sums up one of the most elusive runners in Penn State's early football history. Way was light on his feet. He had to be—he only weighed 125 pounds, a lightweight even in his time.

"He had remarkable stride for a little fellow. I have never seen him tackled by both legs," said one of his teammates.

Way played in 1917, then served in the Army for a year before returning to Penn State for the 1919 and 1920 seasons. A quiet, introverted person, Way usually didn't like to talk about his achievements. But he was particularly proud of being named an All-American in 1920.

One of Way's most memorable moments occurred in the West Virginia Wesleyan game in 1917.

"We won the game in the last minute," Way recalled.

"We packed them up behind their goal line and they took a safety. They were still ahead 7-2. They punted and I ran it back for a TD." Penn State won, 8-7.

Way could "run like a scared rabbit," in his own words. Remarkably, Penn State's "scatback" broke off many of his longest runs by going through the center of the line—usually fullback territory. Why was that?

"I never liked to run the ends, because it was too long a way around," he once said in an interview. "I just liked to run inside. It was more direct that way."

Dancing on the Tanbark

Say the Charleston and you think of the 1920s when the onetime red-hot dance number was all the craze.

It was no less popular at Penn State, but for more than just social dancing. Prior to the 1920 season, coach Hugo Bezdek used the Charleston as part of the team's pre-season training. The idea was to improve the players' footwork.

Said the *New York Times*: "About thirty candidates reported for the Penn State squad, many of whom showed themselves quite proficient in the technique of the dance floor innovation. The players perform[ed] an adaptation of the Charleston in their cleated shoes on the tanbark of the Stock pavilion."

Bezdek took the idea from the West Virginia wrestling team, which, according to the *Times*, "was the first to adopt the jazz dance."

Whether or not there was any correlation, Penn State did waltz away with a 7-0-2 record that season.

Reversing Their Field

Many a football innovation has been born out of accident, or necessity. Take the 1919 season when Hugo Bezdek was coaching at Penn State with Dick Harlow as his assistant.

Harlow once remembered: "A signal was missed and the wing did not take the ball from [quarterback] Harry Robb. Being a smart back, Robb turned toward the line and a huge hole developed.

"This was talked over but nothing was done when the same thing happened again. It was put in as a play."

Thus was the beginning of the fake reverse, a staple in the Penn State attack and one of the popular plays of the 1920s:

It might have been used earlier elsewhere, but Harlow insisted that the first time he had seen a play like that was during that 1919 season at Penn State.

THE "HIG" AND HARD TIMES
1930–1948

Imagine a college football coach keeping his job after seven straight losing seasons. Not likely today. But that's exactly what happened with Bob Higgins at Penn State.

There were extenuating circumstances. When Higgins took over the head coaching position from Hugo Bezdek in 1930, he walked into a bleak situation at Penn State. The combination of the school's "purity campaign" against subsidizing athletes and the Depression had plunged Penn State into one of the darkest periods of its sports history.

As a Penn State player 11 years before, Higgins was applauded as an All-American. Now he was the object of scorn at his own school. Once after a 47-0 loss to Cornell in 1939, Higgins was raked over in print by the *Collegian*, Penn State's student newspaper. Higgins's wife, Virginia, was livid. When her husband coached Penn State to its first victory over Pitt in 20 years at the end of the season, Virginia provided the perfect cap to the season by kicking the *Collegian's* editor in the pants.

Losing to the likes of little Waynesburg College put humility into Higgins. "When you get licked as often as I did in those terrible 1930s, you get over being a tough guy," he said.

But the losing days would soon be forgotten in the 1940s when the "Hig" made winning a habit with old-fashioned power football. Higgins was credited with laying the groundwork for Penn State's defensive giants of later years.

His greatest accomplishment was the 1947 Cotton Bowl team that went undefeated, outscoring opponents 319-27. Steve Suhey and Sam Tamburo keyed a line that helped Penn State establish three national defensive records. The 1947 Nittany Lions were the first to win the Lambert Trophy, annually awarded to the best team in the East, and finished No. 4 in the final Associated Press poll after tying SMU 13-13 in the Cotton Bowl.

Pouring Pepper on the Wounds

Playing Pitt was always a challenge for Penn State in more ways than one. In the old days it was suspected that whenever the Nittany Lions visited the Panthers, Pitt would water down the field to slow Penn State runners. During the Hugo Bezdek era (1918-1929), the Nittany Lions wore long wooden cleats on their shoes to counteract the wet field.

Now it was 1941 and the Nittany Lions were preparing to face their great intrastate rivals at Pitt. As usual, there was a pep rally at State College two days before the game and everyone was fired up, including Penn State coach Bob Higgins.

It was obvious Higgins was aware of Pitt's lawn care tendencies. He was not fazed by it. Stepping up to the microphone, the confident Higgins said:

"It will be no surprise to me if we win. We'll beat Pitt on a wet or dry field—or in the Allegheny River if they want to play there."

The "Hig," as he was known, was right on with his prediction. Penn State tailback Pepper Petrella scored three times as the Nittany Lions romped, 30-7.

Finally Spitting Out the Pitt

When Penn State beat Pittsburgh in 1939, it was a cause for huge celebration on the State College campus. No wonder. Many of the students were barely out of diapers, some not even alive, the last time the Nittany Lions had beaten the Panthers.

From 1920-38, the Panthers held a 14-0-2 edge in the series. The period was so lopsided in Pitt's favor that the game for a while was moved back from its choice spot on Thanksgiving Day to the middle of the season. It was even eliminated from the Penn State schedule for three years.

An inability to beat Penn State's fiercest rival, among other things, ultimately cost Hugo Bezdek his coaching position.

Then came 1939 and Penn State, under long-suffering Bob Higgins, finally whipped Pitt, 10-0.

How excited was everyone on the Penn State campus? Alumni Secretary Ridge Riley wrote in his newsletter: "Penn State's delirious student body last Saturday became so confused that it stormed out on the field and captured its own goalposts and bore them triumphantly down campus to the main gate."

As they say in football, a rivalry isn't life and death—it's more important than that.

State's Waterloo

Whenever Penn State met Pitt, you could usually expect the unexpected. After knocking off the Panthers in 1939, Penn State was favored to beat them again in 1940.

The Panthers were an inferior team that had been booed off the stage at its own pep rally.

So guess what? Naturally, Pitt triumphed over Penn State, 20-7. The loss on the last day of the regular season cost the Nittany Lions an unbeaten year and a probable bowl trip.

It was almost too much to bear for Penn State alumni secretary Ridge Riley. In his weekly *Football Letter*, Riley wrote in the florid Grantland Rice style of the day:

"Within the grimness of Pitt Stadium, Penn State's visions of an undefeated season went up in the murky Pittsburgh sky, and heavy Penn State hearts finished out a weekend in the Smoky City with forced gaiety and dreams of what might have been."

There were some silver linings in the clouds, though, according to Riley.

"Well, anyway, the varsity soccer team finished its eighth consecutive season without defeat."

Buddy, Can You Spare a Dime?

Penn State football was no lark for Bob Higgins in the 1930s. But despite one losing season after another, Higgins never lost his job or his sense of humor.

Higgins liked to tell this story on himself:

"One time, after losing our annual game at Pitt, I approached a Penn State rooter and asked him for a nickle to call a friend. He gave me a disgusted look, tossed me a dime and muttered: 'Here, call both your friends!'"

Tale of the Tape

Before coaching at Penn State, Bob Higgins had played pro football with the Canton Bulldogs. He was constantly reminded, to his everlasting regret, of the time he had to pinch-hit for the legendary Jim Thorpe.

Thorpe, the most popular player of the day and one of the greatest athletes of all time, had failed to appear for one of the games, and the Bulldogs' management didn't want to disappoint the fans. So Higgins was enlisted to impersonate Thorpe.

Higgins was heavily taped up by teammates in order to fill out Thorpe's huge uniform. When Higgins appeared on the field, he probably felt more like an Egyptian mummy than a football player.

He didn't fool the fans, though. When he went back to punt on one play, one of them shouted "Who's that bum in Thorpe's uniform?"

The "bum" only turned out to be one of the most popular football coaches in Penn State history.

A Sizeable Mistake

Win or lose, Bob Higgins always insisted on proper decorum and proper dress for his players, both on and off the field.

Once Higgins chewed out a student manager because a player reported for practice wearing apparently oversized shoes.

"Get this boy a pair of shoes that fit him," Higgins snapped at the student manager. "Get rid of these gunboats."

At which point the player quietly intervened: "Thanks, coach, but these 'gunboats' fit fine. I wear size 14, you see."

The Hig

When he coached at Penn State, Bob Higgins was known as a hands-on guy. After retirement, it was strictly hands off.

For two decades after his retirement in 1948, Higgins lived in the shadow of Beaver Field, always resisting the impulse to second-guess the coaches who followed him. It was greatly appreciated by Rip Engle, who coached from 1950-65.

"I admired Higgins, because after he stepped down he never put a coach on the spot and never tried to make anybody look bad," Engle said.

Not that Higgins didn't occasionally show up for practices. Usually it was with grandchildren on one arm and a dog on the other.

"Who can look for coaching or player mistakes and still watch children?" Higgins would quip.

Socking It to 'Em

The Depression described the nation's economic status in the early 1930s, but it also could have reflected the hard times for Penn State's football program.

After taking over as coach from Hugo Bezdek in 1930, Bob Higgins managed only two winning years in the entire decade.

The 2-8 season in 1931 was the low point, inspiring blistering cartoons in the newspapers. One of them depicted a battered lion with bandages on its body, a disgusted look on its face and its tail tied to a stake in the ground. Clipped to the tail were eight clothespins, each with the name of a team that beat Penn State that year.

"The season was just one sock after another," said the frowning lion.

Go Figure

It isn't unusual today to see women covering college football. In the 1930s, things were different. At that time the males did their best to keep the fair sex out of the press box.

One female who strenuously objected was Betty Starr of the old *Philadelphia Record*. She was covering the Penn State-Lehigh game in 1931 at Franklin Field in Philadelphia.

Even though the game was played for charity—the proceeds going to unemployment funds—the male sports writers were hardly charitable in dealing with Starr.

She apparently tried to crack the press box, but was rebuked. Bored with the game itself, a 31-0 Penn State blowout, she responded with the only weapon she had—sarcasm. The following observation appeared in her story:

"As one person, who stood the blinding drizzle about as long as possible and sought refuge in the covered part of the stand, remarked as she looked up at the multitude of steps leading to the Sacred Press, 'No wonder the sports writers are so lithe and handsome, climbing all those steps must be good for the figure.'"

Dreaming Up a Play

Bob Higgins was so good at inventing exotic plays it was said he could do it in his sleep. One time he literally did that.

Two days before meeting Colgate in 1942 he had a dream about the game.

"It was a rather simple thing," Higgins once remembered. "Our fullback passed sharply to our end, who was standing on the 40-yard line with his back to the Colgate defender. And just as the Colgate man closed in on him, one of our halfbacks drifted by, took the ball on a pass-off and outran the Colgate secondary to the goal line."

The play worked so perfectly in Higgins's dream that he decided to use it in the game.

"It worked just as I had visualized it," Higgins said. "The Colgate boys did just what I had hoped they would do. Our timing was perfect. Everybody cooperated. It was a beautiful thing."

The result was a Penn State touchdown and a 13-10 victory for the Nittany Lions.

Youthful Exuberance

Youth was the hallmark of Penn State's teams during the Second World War. And while they were often successful on the field, they could also drive coach Bob Higgins to distraction with their antics.

Higgins was once riding along the highway for a game at Syracuse when he spotted several of his players—all freshmen —fighting a farmhouse fire.

"Not content to stay on the ground, they were dangling from the roof of a nearby barn, their hands occupied with buckets, and their heads completely barren of everything, including the game on the next day," remembered one Penn State man.

Higgins almost had a heart attack. It wasn't any easier on him once he got his exuberant young players into their hotel rooms. The freshmen had purchased all the chocolate bars in the lobby, tried to talk their way into a jitterbug contest and had risked their limbs by racing full-tilt through the hotel's revolving doors.

Said Higgins: "I hope once the war is over that someone will someday erect a monument to freshman football coaches."

The Name Game

Bob Higgins was one coach who could easily communicate his thoughts to players. Pronouncing their names, however, was entirely something else.

Penn State's 1938 squad had so many unpronounceable names for Higgins that he devised his own shorthand speaking system to address them.

Center Leon Gajecki was one of the tongue twisters for the Nittany Lions football coach. "He couldn't say 'Gajecki,'" remembered Mildred Gajecki, "so he told my husband, 'You're 'Gates.'"

Other jawbreakers for Higgins that season: Frketich, Garbinski, Stravinski and Petrella. Even Morey was too much for the Penn State coach.

So Frketich became Ferguson, Garbinski became Garber, Stravinski became Stevens, Petrella became Pete and Morey became More.

"We had a big tackle named John Michael Leon Kerns, Jr.," Gajecki remembered. "He had an easy Irish name so he didn't have to change it for Higgins."

The Wrong Thing to Say

The great 1947 Penn State team didn't struggle in too many games, but the Nittany Lions found themselves in a real battle with Navy—for a while, anyway. That is, until one of the Midshipmen opened his mouth.

Navy was giving Penn State all it could handle through the first quarter. At one point, Penn State end John Potaklan complimented a Navy lineman on a particularly good block.

"Sure, it was a good block," the Navy player said. "You're playing in the big league today."

When Potaklan came back to the Penn State huddle, he reported what the Navy player had said. It inspired a strong Penn State attack that swept the Navy aside, 20-7.

A Little Sense of Humor

One of the biggest names on the 1947 Penn State team was one of its smallest players—145-pound Elwood Petchell, whom Bob Higgins called "the best back of his weight in the country."

Nevertheless, sports writers still joked about his size. In a program story for the Cotton Bowl that season, *Pittsburgh Press* sports editor Chester L. Smith took the opportunity to take a jab at Penn State's big little man.

"He will be the smallest man on the field, and that, no doubt, includes the water boys," Smith wrote. "Higgins worried about him all the way down until he learned that there were no gopher holes in Dallas."

Never mind the jokes. Petchell was practically the whole offensive show for Penn State against SMU. He threw two touchdown passes, completed seven throws for 93 yards and rushed for 25 more as the Nittany Lions tied the powerful Mustangs, 13-13.

The Persistent Petchell

Another story about the pocket-size Petchell:

Once he tried to tackle a Navy player, but wound up as a piggyback rider, because he simply wasn't strong enough to bring him down.

As he passed the Penn State bench on the back of the runner, Petchell shouted to coach Bob Higgins: "Hi, ho, Silver!"

Whistling in the Wind

Along with the irrepressible Petchell, the 1948 Penn State team featured another free spirit in running back Fran Rogel. He was nicknamed "Punchy," because he appeared oblivious to everything on the field—including the referee's whistle.

He was usually the last one to hear it when a play was blown dead.

"I never hear anything on the field except signals," he would say.

Rogel constantly complained about the referee's "fast whistle." One time as he walked back to the huddle after another of his irrepressible runs, he pulled at the referee's sleeve.

"Hey, mister, don't blow that thing so fast," Rogel told him. "I'm never down."

He Could Have Kicked Himself

Ed Czekaj did a lot of good things as a football player and athletic director at Penn State. Nevertheless, he is also remembered for the missed extra point in the 1948 Cotton Bowl that would have given the Nittany Lions the victory.

"No matter where I go, they always remember that," Czekaj once recalled of the 13-13 tie in Dallas.

Wishing to console his blond kicker after he missed the crucial extra point, Bob Higgins approached Czekaj and asked: "Did you think your kick was good, Ed?"

"I don't know, coach," Czekaj responded. "You always told me to keep my head down."

Ripping Open
a New Era
1950–1965

With the launching of Sputnik by the Soviet Union, a new era dawned. The space race was on, and the United States had every intention of winning it.

Meanwhile, a new era was also dawning at Penn State with Rip Engle and a kid coach named Joe Paterno. Engle had come to State College from Brown University, bringing Paterno along to coach the quarterbacks. It was a good thing, too. Engle had yet to meet anyone else on his staff.

One of the stipulations of Engle's new job was that he retain the entire Penn State coaching staff, including former head coach Joe Bedenk. Engle entered the position "with a lot of misgivings."

"I had never met these coaches," he said. "They were all Single Wing coaches. The whole staff that was here had been here long before me—and then Joe (Paterno) had never coached. It was a pretty precarious situation, and I just wondered how smart I was."

Smarter than he thought, as it turned out. It would not be long before Engle, with the help of a loyal coaching staff, would make his mark at Penn State. During his 16 seasons the Nittany Lions played in four bowl games—twice as many as the rest of the Penn State teams did prior to 1950. The Lions won three of them, starting a trend of bowl successes that would continue under Paterno.

Some of the players who helped make Penn State a success during this time: Sam Valentine, Rich Lucas, Bob Mitinger, Dave Robinson, Roger Kochman and Glenn Ressler.

Showing His True Colors

From 1954 to 1956, they were mortal enemies on a football field. Who would have figured Dan Radakovich and Joe Walton would wind up many years later working in harmony as coaching colleagues? Well, to a point.

Radakovich played for Penn State as a linebacker. Walton was a defensive end and tight end for Pitt. The two went head to head on three occasions during a time when the Penn State-Pitt series was as intense as it ever was.

Fast forward to the '90s. The two former adversaries were now reunited as coaches for the newly established Robert Morris College football team.

. Radakovich was delighted to note that the Robert Morris's school colors were blue and white, same as they are at Penn State. Pitt loyalist Walton, on the other hand, refused to coach a team with those colors.

"As head coach, I added a little red so we wouldn't be the same as Penn State," he said.

Radakovich wasn't entirely thrilled with the change. But there was little he could complain about. He certainly wasn't going to argue against red, white and blue.

Paternally Paterno

Hall of Famer Dave Robinson had the pleasure of playing for two legendary coaches—Joe Paterno in college and Vince Lombardi in the pros. Well, it wasn't always a pleasure.

Penn State coach Rip Engle with (left to right) end Dave Robinson, tackle Chuck Sieminski and halfback Roger Kochman.

"You would fear both men—the way you would fear your father," Robinson once remembered. "You know that your father will do anything for you, but if you mess up, you know you will be punished for it. That's how Vince and Joe were."

And like most fathers, Paterno was protective. One story in particular brought home the point.

It was 1962 and the Nittany Lions were in Florida for the Gator Bowl. Robinson was an All-America linebacker and receiver. He was also the only black on Penn State's traveling squad.

When the Nittany Lions stopped at an Orlando restaurant for lunch one day, the restaurant manager told them they didn't serve blacks. Head coach Rip Engle was incensed. If Robinson couldn't eat there, then none of the Penn State players would eat there.

Engle then gave each player lunch money and told him to find food elsewhere. For the moment, Robinson was relieved. Then he wasn't. "What good is this expense money if no one's going to let me in and eat?" he thought.

Enter Paterno. Then Penn State's offensive coordinator, Paterno took Robinson to a coffee shop.

"You know, I had the feeling that if they threw me out, they were going to have to throw out Joe, too," Robinson said.

Of course they didn't. Robinson and Paterno enjoyed lunch together.

Good Cop, Bad Cop

Rip Engle was the coach, Joe Paterno the assistant. To Bob Mitinger, they both got the job done, but in different ways.

"Rip Engle never got mad," remembered Mitinger, who played both the offensive and defensive end positions at Penn State from 1959-61.

Paterno, on the other hand, was more intense and more vocal. Much more.

"Paterno would get mad," Mitinger said. "He would crack the whip."

They were not so different in other ways. After taking over for Engle as head coach in 1966, Paterno continued Engle's philosophy emphasizing the student athlete.

"Many of the ideals that Joe espouses today are the ideals that Rip Engle recruited me with," Mitinger said in a 1987

Rip Engle had Something in common with Jack Kennedy.

interview. "When he came into my living room my senior year in high school [at Greensburg High School near Pittsburgh], he emphasized academics over athletics. He came off as a perfect gentlemen."

Mitinger must have listened closely. Today he is a lawyer in State College.

Riverboat Richie

The term "triple threat" conjures up visions of old-time football when a single player did it all: punt, pass and run.

But a "quadruple threat?" Put quarterback Rich Lucas in that category.

Lucas had a memorable senior year at Penn State in 1959: He passed for 913 yards and five touchdowns, rushed for 325 yards, punted 20 times for a 34-yard average and on defense intercepted five passes for 114 yards.

Coach Rip Engle liked Lucas for his "gambling ability— he likes to take chances." Penn State's sports information department further projected Lucas's image as a gambler. The publicists set up a stock photo of the player dressed in costume like the traditional riverboat gambler: sleeves pinched back by garters, a high-top hat jauntily cocked to one side and a deck of cards in hand.

Lucas showed a gambler's instincts early in his Penn State career when the Nittany Lions were playing West Virginia. Late in the first half, the Nittany Lions had a fourth and five and Lucas dropped back to punt.

At least that's what everyone thought—including Engle. Lucas, however, kept the ball and raced 25 yards for a first down.

Actually, Engle had ordered Lucas to punt on that play but was overturned by the risk-taking quarterback.

"When he sends in a play," Lucas said of Engle, "I treat it as a suggestion."

Warmed-Over Duck

The 1960 Liberty Bowl in Philadelphia will go down as a special game in Penn State football history, and not only because the Nittany Lions beat Oregon, 41-12.

Believe it or not—pay attention, Mr. Ripley—it was the first time that heaters were used on the sidelines of a football game. At least that's what newspapers reported.

It was probably one of the first games as well to enlist the aid of city government to get the field in shape for the Dec. 17 contest. The city provided snowplows to clean out 14 inches of snow that had dropped on the field of Philadelphia Municipal Stadium a few days before the game.

"I guess I was out there shoveling with everyone else," said A. F. "Bud" Dudley, the bowl's founder and executive director. "It was disheartening, to say the least."

Not as disheartening as the condition of the sidelines, however. About a dozen infrared lamps were set up a couple of feet over the heads of the players on the benches. They were supposed to keep them comfortable in the face of 30-degree temperatures and 20-mile-per-hour winds.

"Instead the players turned medium rare," quipped one newspaperman. "After a quarter or so, they felt as if they had been sitting on the beach in Florida."

The lights also toasted the sidelines, turning that part of the field into a mud bath.

"It became a quagmire," Dudley once remembered. "No one had ever tried a heater at a game. I've had a lot of firsts, some good, some bad."

Oh, well. You win some, you lose some and some wash away with the tide.

Presidential Connections

On the way south to train for the 1962 Gator Bowl, the Penn State football team stopped off at the White House.

There the team presented President Kennedy with an autographed football and a model of the Nittany Lion. The players were familiar with Kennedy's love of sports, but perhaps unaware that he had football connections with Penn State coach Rip Engle.

Turned out that Kennedy and Engle both played for Dick Harlow—Kennedy when he was on the freshman and JV squads at Harvard and Engle when he played at Penn State.

Not only that, Kennedy's brother, attorney general Robert F. Kennedy, also was on the Harvard team when Harlow coached the Crimson.

The White House connections with Engle didn't stop there. As Kennedy greeted Engle and the Nittany Lions outside of his office, he asked Kenneth O'Donnell, the President's appointment secretary, to join the group. O'Donnell, a former Harvard standout, had once played against an Engle-coached team at Brown.

Making a Spectacle of Himself

Lenny Moore was not only one of the greatest running backs in Penn State history, but a trailblazer for blacks in college football.

"Lenny was the first [black] that played in the Texas Christian [University] stadium," Joe Paterno remembered.

That was 1954, when Penn State traveled to Texas to play the TCU Horned Frogs. Because blacks were not allowed in local hotels at that time, the Penn State team was forced to stay at a ranch outside of Fort Worth.

Paterno remembered that Moore was a little apprehensive about the trip, Penn State's first to Texas to play football.

"It's come down as truth, don't know how true, but Lenny was getting on the plane in Pittsburgh [for the team charter flight to Texas]," Paterno recalled.

Penn State coach Rip (Engle) spotted Moore wearing a pair of sunglasses.

"Rip said, 'Hey, Lenny, what are you doing? You hot-dogging it wearing sunglasses?', or whatever the term was in those days.

Lenny Moore was a trailblazer for blacks in college football.

"Lenny said, 'No, coach, but when I travel in the south, I travel incognito.'"

Fellow Traveler

For Joe Paterno, working with Rip Engle was one of the great joys of his life. He especially enjoyed traveling with Engle on recruiting trips.

"Rip was a great traveler," Paterno once remembered of his boss who coached at Penn State from 1950-65. "Rip always liked to stop."

And stay.

One time Paterno and Engle took off on a recruiting mission that went through North Carolina.

"Instead of going the regular way, we went right through the Smokies," Paterno recalled. "It was beautiful, but desolate. We were getting hungry so we saw a place called 'Dad's Place' and we stopped. We stopped Rip's big Cadillac."

Out of the front door rolled six beer cans. The owner was cleaning up.

"We go in and there are some guys sitting in the corner. Rip says, 'How far's Asheville?' One guy says, 'Ain't ever been there before.' Another guy says, 'I was there about 20 years ago. Say, about 130 miles.'"

Some time later, Engle and Paterno were still holding down a table. And holding court.

"You couldn't get Rip out of that place," Paterno remembered. "He just wanted to talk to them. He just enjoyed that kind of stuff. When he traveled, he talked to everybody."

Moore, or Less

Rip Engle's early teams at Penn State in the 1950s featured explosive Lenny Moore, one of Penn State's all-time great halfbacks.

Moore's singular presence alone changed Penn State's offensive orientation from passing to running. From 1953-55 at Penn State, the high-stepping Moore was one of the most feared running backs in the country.

When Penn State faced Pitt in 1954, the Panthers were naturally totally geared up to stop Moore. But for one of the few times that anyone could remember, Engle used Moore strictly as a decoy against Pitt. Penn State won, 13-0.

After the game, Engle apologized to Moore for not giving him a chance to break several Eastern rushing records. Moore didn't seem to mind.

"Coach," he said, "I had a wonderful time in there to-day. Faking is much easier on you."

As it was, Moore's 1,082 yards were good enough for a single-season rushing record at Penn State. At the time, it surpassed Shorty Miller's record set in 1912.

A Rosey Outlook

His nickname was "Rosey" and it was apropos. Roosevelt Grier was always looking at the world through rose-colored glasses.

"He had a sense of humor that contributed greatly to our squad morale," coach Rip Engle once remembered of Grier, a standout lineman from 1951-54. "He always knew when to insert a little humor into a dull practice session or give someone a lift when it was needed most."

Engle's favorite "Rosey" story happened long after the big tackle had left Penn State for the pros. Engle had undergone surgery when he received a get-well card. It said:

"Dear Rip, you can't make the club sitting in the tub. Get well."

The card was signed by Grier.

Engle pointed out: "I had always insisted to the squad that you can never make the team sitting in the training room or in the whirlpool bath."

Fifteen years later, Grier turned it around on Engle.

Snow Job

Talk about a team not showing up. The Nittany Lions literally almost didn't for their 1953 clash with Fordham.

As was customary on the eve of a home game, Rip Engle took his players by bus to a mountain retreat some 20 miles from State College. A heavy snow was already falling, causing concern for Engle and his staff. The head coach was up half the night, worried about what travel problems he might face in the morning.

Penn State's athletic office was worried, too, particularly after the heavy snow continued ferociously after daybreak. And worried even more when it was learned the team bus was stuck in snowy back roads and not able to get back into the camp.

Assistant coaches Joe Paterno and Jim O'Hora, fortified with a good breakfast, went out in search of the missing bus. After a one-mile jog in their sweatsuits, they returned cold and wet—and empty-handed.

Now Engle was really nervous. He instructed two rifle-armed cooks to serve as lookouts. If and when the bus should appear, the cooks were ordered to fire shots.

Then Engle sent out an advance contingent—11 players least likely to play—to clear a path for the regulars. The players fell in line, with Paterno and O'Hora holding up the rear. This disheveled group trundled through the snow looking for the lost bus and was much the worse for wear when a rifle shot rang out. The bus had been found!

The tired players boarded the bus and painstakingly made their way to Beaver Field, arriving just about the time of the scheduled kickoff. Officials had decided to play the game after the field had been cleared following the 10-inch snowfall.

While his players quickly dressed, Engle sought out Fordham coach Ed Danowski and apologized for being late. He then asked Danowski if he didn't mind starting the game a half-hour later. The Fordham coach graciously consented.

As Engle was about to leave, Danowski asked: "By the way, what did you say the name of the camp was?"

"Camp Hate-to-Leave-It," responded a humorless Engle before retiring to his own locker room.

Penn State somehow managed to win, 28-21.

Stating His Case

Penn State's 7-6 victory at Ohio State in 1956 was one of the Nittany Lions' greatest moments under Rip Engle. As quarterback Milt Plum once remembered: "We were underdogs by four touchdowns and everyone in Columbus thought we were coming in just to sell popcorn. But we gave 110 percent and it was the best feeling of winning I've ever had."

All the rest of the Penn State players felt the same way. And their giddy feeling carried over for most of them to the following week's game against West Virginia.

During the West Virginia game, the public address announcer reported that Ohio State had taken an early lead over Wisconsin. A Penn State player, still enjoying that triumph over Ohio State, interrupted Plum's huddle to ask if everyone had heard the news.

Sam Valentine, Penn State's All-America guard, reacted sharply to the interruption.

"Listen, men, this is the West Virginia game and we don't have it won yet," Valentine said. "Let's forget that Ohio State game."

The Lions put their minds to the task at hand and whipped West Virginia, 16-6.

Striking It Rich

During his time at Penn State, Rich Lucas did it all for the Nittany Lions—pass, punt and play defense with style. In 1959, the daring play-caller from Glassport, Pennsylvania, was named to several All-America teams.

He was one of Rip Engle's favorite players. "He looked like a choir boy, but he had murder in his heart when he played football," Engle once said of the quarterback with nerves of steel and a lucky gambler's instinct.

If not for a chance discovery, though, Lucas might never have played for Penn State.

Engle and his staff were once viewing a game film between two Pennsylvania high schools. Engle was interested in scouting Bethel High School quarterback Jerry Eisamen. But as the film went on, Eisamen was constantly being upstaged by a player from Glassport High School. He was making most of the tackles, intercepting passes and just stealing the show.

"What's that kid's name?" Engle asked.

"It's Lucas—Richie Lucas," said backfield coach Joe Paterno.

"Let's run the film over again and see what he does on defense," Engle said.

Engle was so impressed that he gave up the hunt for Eisamen and went after Lucas, who became one of the great players in Penn State history. Eisamen wound up at Kentucky.

Of Mules and Men

A football coach who never swore, wore blue Bermuda shorts, tennis shoes with no socks and a pink sailor's hat. That was one of the images that stayed with Bob Mitinger long after he had played for kindhearted Rip Engle.

"Whenever you'd make a mistake, Engle would put his arm around you and say, 'God love you, son. Surely you can give a little better effort than that,'" recalled Mitinger, an All-America end for Penn State in 1961.

Engle literally emerged from the dark into the light when he found the world of football as a freshman in college. Prior to that, he had worked in the Pennsylvania coal mines. So he was appreciative of everything he got.

"I've come from as far down as some people can come," Engle once said in an interview.

Engle said he learned a lot about life from driving a mule in the mines at age 14.

"That's the most prominent mule I ever knew," he said. "That mule taught me a lot of lessons. He was the greatest mule—a small mule—but I always thought, 'What a wonderful animal.' He was always happy working. He could outwork all the rest of the mules put together. That mule taught me how to work."

Engle went to Blue Ridge College in Maryland and played in the first football game he saw. Later he starred at Western Maryland College, playing under former Penn State coach Dick Harlow. It was Harlow who steered Engle into coaching.

"I never expected to be a coach," Engle said. "I got out of school right after the Depression and that was the only kind of job I could get. Coach Harlow had two jobs for me coaching, and I couldn't find another job to save me. Otherwise I would have never been a coach."

It was a good thing for Penn State. After successes on the high school level and then Brown University, Engle was hired for Penn State in 1950. In the next 15 years, Engle built Penn State into a national power.

He knew when to leave, too. And he left Penn State wanting more.

"I felt it. When football began to lose its charm and began to lose its fun, I went to the president of the school [Dr. Eric A. Walker], and said I wanted to leave. And he said, 'Well, you can still be our coach five more years.' And I said, 'Yes, that's when I want to get out—when I can still be your coach.'"

Are You Talking to Me?

While Engle rarely used sharp language with his players, the same couldn't always be said of his staff. One such assistant with a sharp tongue was J.T. White, who coached at Penn State from 1954-79.

"He always called people 'Knucklehead,'" Mitinger once remembered. "In my senior year, he called me by my first name, and I didn't know who he was talking to."

The All-Name Team

Mention Rip Engle and you immediately think of his connection to Penn State football. But Engle had quite a bit of previous success, including the time he spent at Brown University.

It was in 1944 that Brown pulled off an upset of Colgate that Engle called "one of my earliest thrills." Relying on a series of quick traps and quarterback-keeper plays, Brown upset Colgate 32-20. Brown had not beaten Colgate for 20 years and had never defeated an Andy Kerr-coached team.

"We had a group consisting of 17-year-olds and wartime rejects," Engle once recalled, "and it was a lean year for victories."

"On our team that day we had Pat O'Brien at quarterback, Roger Williams at wingback, Tommy Dorsey at halfback, and Dick Tracy at end. A very imposing list of celebrities it was—but they weren't the originals."

NOT JUST ANOTHER JOE
1966–1979

In an era of social movement and dramatic changes in America, Penn State also made a change that would have an impact on its football program.

Rip Engle retired after the 1965 season, handing the head coaching job to Joe Paterno. A longtime assistant in charge of quarterbacks, Paterno had achieved prominence for his development of such players as Richie Lucas, Milt Plum, Al Jacks, Tony Rados, Dick Hoak, Galen Hall and Pete Liske.

"I knew that Joe would become an outstanding coach," Engle said once in an interview. "I knew even when I came here that he had a keen football mind. His leadership and competitive attitude made him a fine quarterback, and when I came to Penn State in 1950, he was the one person I brought along even though he had just graduated from college. I was aware even then of his potential as a fine coach."

Paterno, the 14th coach in Penn State history, began his career inauspiciously with a 5-5 record in 1966. There was nothing mediocre about Penn State football after that. The late 1960s produced some extraordinary teams and extraordinary moments, including an exciting 15-14 victory over Kansas in the Orange Bowl to cap an 11-0 season.

Winning seasons, victories in bowls and national rankings became a regularity for Paterno-coached teams after that. A moment in the Orange Bowl game against Kansas seemed to sum up Paterno's philosophy of life, liberty and the pursuit of the football.

After Penn State pulled within 14-13 with a late touchdown, the safe thing would have been to kick the extra point for the tie. Paterno instead went for the riskier two-point conversion to win the game.

"I've always preached to my boys that there's one thing I want you to do and this is don't ever be afraid to lose," Paterno said. "If you're afraid to lose, you don't have a chance of winning."

Socks Up, Boss

Joe Paterno's coaching success at Penn State has long overshadowed the fact that he himself was a pretty good college quarterback.

In the late 1940s, he starred in the same backfield at Brown with his younger brother, George. In physical stature, the two hardly looked like brothers—Joe bespectacled and skinny at QB and George broad and powerful at halfback. In two years together, they led Brown to a 15-3 overall record.

"He couldn't even keep his socks up," George once remembered of his rail-thin brother. "I told him the only play he needed to remember was that one where he handed off to me."

Keeping a Promise

When Joe Paterno recruited offensive tackle Ron Heller in the early 1980s, he promised his mother and father he would get their son an education.

Heller had different priorities, like playing pro ball. In his final semester at Penn State, Heller didn't give much thought to his studies and finished with four Ds and an F. He failed to graduate.

Not graduating was the furthest thing from Heller's mind when he was starting as a rookie for the Tampa Bay Buccaneers. Until a letter arrived at his parents' house from Paterno that made him think about school again.

Paterno wrote a five-page handwritten letter of apology saying he had "failed" in his promise to get Ron a college education. Heller remembered seeing tears welling in his father's eyes as he read the letter.

Ron Heller wondered: "What does he care about me for? I've got nothing to do for him any more."

He went back to school and graduated.

No Presidential Pardon

Not many college football coaches are invited to make the commencement address at their school. Not many take a jab at the President of the United States in the speech, either. In 1973, Joe Paterno took the opportunity to do so while addressing the graduating class at Penn State.

It all started when in 1969, Texas had beaten Arkansas in a battle of unbeatens with President Nixon in attendance. After the game, Nixon visited the winners' locker room. The nation's "Number 1" sports fan handed a "Number 1" plaque to the Longhorns while millions watched on national television, declaring them national champions.

This was naturally met with outrage at Penn State, which also happened to be undefeated. Paterno, feeling that the Nittany Lions had been insulted by no less than the leader of the Free World, reacted in kind.

When Nixon tried to assuage Paterno with a plaque for having the nation's longest winning streak, the Penn State coach refused it. Why should he accept it? After all, Penn State already owned the streak—29 games heading into the Orange Bowl! Paterno was even unhappier when Penn State finished No. 2 to Texas in the final polls, despite a victory over Missouri in the Orange Bowl to cap a perfect 12-0 season.

At the commencement address in the spring of 1973, Paterno hadn't forgotten the slight by Nixon. One of the early remarks in Paterno's speech:

"I'd like to know, how could the President know so little about Watergate in 1973 and so much about college football in 1969?"

Nixing It

One week after the controversy with Penn State, Nixon was in New York to receive an award for his contributions to college football.

While accepting his gold medal award at the Waldorf Astoria, Nixon admitted that he had indeed stuck his foot in his mouth by declaring Texas the top team in the country. He said he was thinking of suggesting that a college "super bowl" be played after the bowl games to decide the true national champion.

"But I was in deep enough already," the president said, "so I decided to skip it."

Twelve Angry Men

The 1969 Orange Bowl was a classic matchup made in football heaven: Kansas's freewheeling offense against Penn State's strong defense.

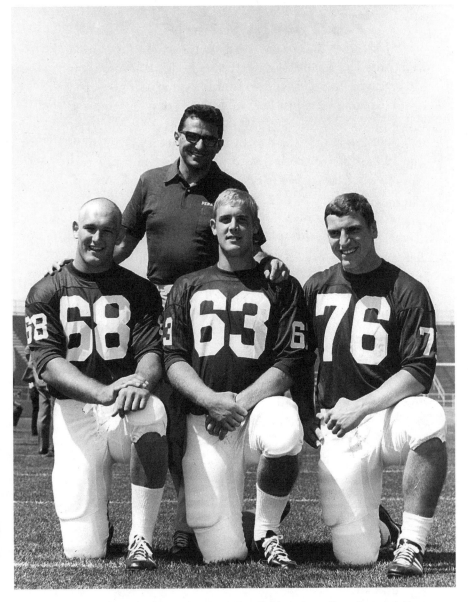

Mike Reid (left) starred on the field and on the stage at Penn State. Also in the picture are teammates Terry Jackson and Steve Smear, backed by Joe Paterno.

"If I had to make a guess, I'd say this might turn into a wild game," said Kansas coach Pepper Rodgers, whose team had averaged 38 points and 442 yards a game.

He had no idea just how wild it was going to get at the end.

Kansas was on its way to an almost certain 14-7 victory. The Jayhawks had the ball with a first down and just two minutes left. All they had to do was run out the clock. A snap, right?

Well, maybe not.

The Jayhawks' first play was stopped at the line of scrimmage. Then Penn State defensive tackle Mike Reid threw Kansas quarterback Bobby Douglass for losses of six and seven yards on the next two plays.

The Jayhawks' punt on fourth down was partially blocked by Neil Smith, giving Penn State the ball on the 50-yard line with 1:16 left.

The Nittany Lions were expected to throw short sideline passes where the receiver could step out of bounds and stop the clock. But in the huddle, halfback Bob Campbell told quarterback Chuck Burkhart: "Throw downfield for the left goalpost. I'll be there."

Burkhart did, and Campbell hauled in the pass behind a leaping Kansas defender. Campbell went for 47 yards before he was downed on the Kansas three-yard line.

The Nittany Lions, who had held opponents to less than 11 points a game in their 10-0 season, were now relying on their less-appreciated offense to win.

On the sidelines, Joe Paterno was drawing up three plays for Burkhart.

"Chuck was positively the coolest guy around," Paterno remembered. "He kept telling me, 'We'll win, Coach. Don't worry.' It was great, but sometimes I wonder if he has enough talent to be all THAT cocky."

Fullback Tom Cherry tried the middle twice. No luck. On third down, Burkhart was then supposed to hand off to Charlie Pittman into the line, a play called "56 Scissors." But Burkhart changed the play at the last second, faked a handoff to the surprised Pittman and bootlegged around left end for his first rushing touchdown at Penn State.

The Nittany Lions were now within one point at 14-13. A kick for the extra point would tie it. In true Paterno fashion, he rejected the idea. He was going for the two-point conversion. He wanted a win, not a tie. "If we couldn't win, we'd lose," he said.

It didn't seem like the best idea when Burkhart's pass to Campbell was knocked away. The Kansas players began to celebrate the apparent 14-13 win.

But—hold on—a flag was on the ground. A penalty was called against the Jayhawks—they had 12 men on the field instead of the legal 11. As films would show later, the Jayhawks actually had played with 12 men on all four plays, including Burkhart's touchdown run.

A second chance for Penn State. This time, from the one-and-a-half-yard line, Campbell raced around left end for the two-point conversion and an exciting 15-14 Penn State victory.

"We turned what would have been a dull win for us into an exciting win for them," Rodgers said.

And arguably the most miraculous finish in Penn State football history.

A Present for Joey

It was before the West Virginia game in 1973 and John Cappelletti had a special birthday request from his 11-year-old brother, Joey: Would he score four touchdowns for him?

A big order for Cappelletti, even though the Penn State running back was one of the top candidates for the Heisman Trophy. But Cappelletti promised four TDS as a present to his brother, who had been stricken with leukemia.

Against West Virginia, Cappelletti scored one touchdown after another. By the time he was finished for the day, he had scored three times and Penn State had piled up an insurmountable lead. Cappelletti retired to the bench while the second-stringers mopped up.

Then Cappelletti's friend, Eddie O'Neil, found Joe Paterno's ear. He told the coach about Cappelletti's promise to score four touchdowns for his sick brother. Into the game once more went Cappelletti, who scored on a two-yard run for his fourth TD in the Nittany Lions' 62-14 romp.

A couple of weeks later, before Penn State faced Ohio University, Cappelletti received the same request from his brother. He delivered four more TDs.

Cappelletti wound up with 17 touchdowns that season. He wasn't very big on personal stats. But it's likely when he was dedicating his Heisman Trophy to Joey at the end of the season, he remembered at least eight of his TD runs.

Joey's Heisman

On a December night in 1973, a large crowd gathered in a New York hotel ballroom to hear the latest Heisman Trophy winner make his acceptance speech.

Since the award for college football's top player was initiated in 1939, it had generally been a tradition for the winners to say a few words.

Many of these speeches were hardly memorable. The audience who listened to John Cappelletti's speech won't soon forget it.

At first the Penn State running back did all the usual things that the winners do: he thanked his teammates, his coach, and his mother and father.

Then he mentioned Joey, his younger brother who had been stricken with leukemia. His voice wavered and tears streamed down his face as 4,000 people sat with rapt attention.

"They say I've shown courage on the football field," Cappelletti said. "But for me, it's only on the field and only in the fall. Joey lives with pain all the time. His courage is round the clock.

"I want him to have this trophy. It's more his than mine, because he's been such an inspiration to me."

Everyone in the room was touched. Many in the audience had tears in their eyes by the time Cappelletti had finished. It was such a moving speech that Bishop Fulton J. Sheen decided to forego his usual benediction.

"Tonight you have heard a speech from the heart, not the lips," Sheen told the crowd. "I was supposed to pronounce the blessing, but you don't need a blessing tonight. God has blessed you in the person of John Cappelletti."

Cappelletti played 11 years in the NFL and then went into the construction business in California. He named one of his four sons after Joey, who died in 1976.

Joe vs. the Volcano

For a number of reasons, Joe Paterno was looking forward to facing Ohio State in 1978. Number one, he would be matching wits with volcanic coaching legend Woody Hayes. Number two, he felt his Penn State team had a good chance of winning, even in the daunting surroundings of the Buckeyes' 88,000-seat stadium.

In the week leading up to the game, Paterno recalled a clinic he and Hayes had attended a couple of years before. "Two days in a row, I noticed Woody eating by himself in the restaurant," Paterno said. "I went over and sat with him, to be sociable. As soon as I sat down, he began lecturing me on what I was doing wrong."

But that weekend at Columbus, Paterno seemed to do everything right. There wasn't much Hayes could find wrong with Penn State after the Nittany Lions beat his Buckeyes, 19-0.

Cutting Comment

The Penn State football coaching staff of the late 1970s was as animated and intense as any that ever served Joe Paterno.

Receiving coach Booker Brooks continually stated his case for a more aggressive passing attack and defensive coach Jerry Sandusky was just as passionate about his players on the other side of the ball.

Then there was offensive line coach Dick Anderson, perhaps the most animated and intense of all. Anderson constantly suffered over the play of his linemen, never happy with the results.

One day Anderson stayed in the shower a little longer than usual and Paterno stuck in his head.

"What are you doing in there, Dick," Paterno said, "slashing your wrists?"

A Million Reasons to Go, One to Stay

For Joe Paterno, money isn't everything. Except for a brief moment when it turned his head. And therein lies the intriguing story of how he once cut his ties with Penn State and took a pro coaching job—but not for long.

This was in the early seventies, after Paterno had made some noise with a couple of unbeaten teams and victories in major bowls.

The call came from Billy Sullivan, owner of the down-trodden New England Patriots: Would Paterno take over the football operation and try to turn his team around?

Sullivan not only offered Paterno complete control of the Patriots as coach and general manager, but also offered him a unprecedented amount of money—more than one million dollars over five years.

The offer was staggering. Remember, this was a time when the dollar had more value, and there were far fewer millionaires in the pre-technology world.

Paterno had always been an idealist. He had gone into football coaching to make a difference in the lives of young men. He considered himself not just a coach, but a teacher. His so-called "Grand Experiment" at Penn State emphasizing the student athlete had been working quite well, thank you. Now he was being tempted to change the direction of his work—actually his philosophy—in exchange for lifetime security for himself and his family.

All of a sudden, Paterno envisioned himself leading the Patriots into the Super Bowl within four or five years. He sat down with his wife, Sue, and made lists. One was headed "Go" and another headed "Stay."

"They all kept coming up 'go,'" Paterno said in a magazine interview. "Money, Cape Cod, security, continued rural living for the kids, excitement, a tremendous coaching challenge. We made the lists over and over. 'Stay' finished behind all the time."

There was simply no choice for Paterno. He accepted Sullivan's offer.

The Paternos went to sleep that night certain they had made the right choice.

But when they woke up the next day, there were still questions in Paterno's mind. Had he really made the right choice? He wasn't 100 percent sure. Back to the drawing board went Paterno with his wife, questioning his own motives.

"After telling Billy Sullivan yes, I started wondering what the hell I had done. I began to realize that all I'd prove at New England was that I could coach a good football team both with college kids and with pros. What's that prove?"

Paterno still thought of himself as a teacher. That was much easier to do on the college level than it was in the National Football League.

"By the time I finally dissected my decision to go to New England, I realized the only reason I accepted the job—the only one—was the money," Paterno said. "I was flattered by the dough. Period."

On second thought, Paterno decided to stay at Penn State. He canceled the deal with the Patriots.

Paterno later kidded his wife.

"You went to bed with a millionaire and woke up a pauper."

Widespread Acclaim

Paterno's decision to turn down a million dollar-plus offer from the New England Patriots in the early 1970s did not go completely unrewarded.

At University Park, Paterno was given a testimonial dinner, and enough money was raised to send him and his wife to Europe and buy them a new car.

Political Punter?

President Paterno? That may not seem so farfetched when you consider Joe Paterno's widespread popularity as a college football icon and his interest in politics.

In truth, Paterno admittedly would have gone into politics had he not become a football coach. He was actually thinking about a career in law before joining Rip Engle on the Penn State coaching staff in 1950.

"I've always been fascinated by politics," Paterno said in a magazine interview in the early 1970s. "There's a similarity between good politics and good football—you can't do either without a lot of early work, preparation."

Paterno makes no secret about his Republican affiliation.

"My father did a lot of legwork for the Democrats in Brooklyn when I was a kid," Paterno said. "God, he'd roll over in his grave if he knew I was a registered Republican."

Identity Problem

Tony Petruccio, a fine middle guard at Penn State in the 1970s, had also been recruited by Ohio State. He tells why he chose the Nittany Lions:

"[Ohio State coach Woody] Hayes had me and a Puerto Rican guy in at the same time. I thought I was doing OK, but when I was getting ready to leave he put his arm on my shoulder and said, 'Well, Chico, I'm glad you could make it.'

"I knew then I wasn't interested in Ohio State."

A Shorter Walk

Just because Matt Suhey had deep family ties to Penn State didn't necessarily mean he would play football for the Nittany Lions.

In fact the grandson of former football coach Bob Higgins and the son of All-America guard Steve Suhey was seriously considering Ohio State when the Buckeyes recruited him in the 1970s.

But a couple of things changed his mind in favor of Penn State. For one thing, he loved the involvement in sports of everyone on campus— including the professors.

He said one of those who taught government described "lobbying" as "the kind of thing Woody Hayes and Joe Paterno did when they were trying to get Matt Suhey."

The point that sold him on Penn State, he said, was more practical, though. Suhey had just come back to the tight campus at University Park after a visit to the sprawling Ohio State campus.

"I realized the difference," he said. "A five-minute walk."

Suhey, of course, would go on to glory as one of the best fullbacks in Penn State history.

Film at Eleven

Like any successful college football coach, Joe Paterno spends a lot of time watching films of his opponent in preparation for upcoming games.

It was no different before Penn State pulled into a Columbus motel for a game against Ohio State in 1978. Paterno made sure his players got a nine o'clock snack before they went to their rooms for a good night's sleep.

Then he went to the hospitality room to join a few newspapermen, who were watching the Muhammad Ali-Michael Spinks fight.

The fight went the limit. When it was over, Paterno was asked by one reporter how he scored it.

"Not till he sees the films," cracked another.

Unappreciative

It would be hard to find a quarterback that worked as hard as Chuck Fusina at Penn State in the 1970s. Each year after football season ended, it was only the beginning for the McKees Rocks, Pennsylvania, native.

"I took a projector home with me and ran game films over and over," Fusina said. "I'd sit there in the dark and watch myself throwing interceptions and I'd see what I should have been doing."

Fusina also practiced throwing pass routes to a friend, hour after hour, day after day. And of course he put to memory the Penn State playbook, which featured 13 different offensive sets and 50-60 plays.

"My buddy and that projecter, they were very relieved when it was time to go back to school," Fusina said.

The dedication paid off for Fusina, who set many Penn State passing records in his time and turned the Nittany Lions into a formidable aerial power.

One of the most popular football players ever at Penn State, Fusina received more than his share of fan mail. Most of it came from young fans, and most of it was flattering.

However, Fusina once remembered one letter that wasn't.

"One kid told me he saw me play and decided he wanted to be a quarterback because he didn't want to work too hard."

Bad Beginning, Good Ending

It was one of those brief exchanges between coach and player on the sidelines, a story within the story of a heated football game. Penn State was playing Pitt in a nationally televised battle in 1974 for the mythical Eastern championship.

Penn State split end Jim Easie had just fumbled a punt for the second time in the game, setting up a touchdown for Pitt.

When Easie returned to the Penn State bench, there was no finger pointing, no signs of disapproval from anyone. In fact, players on the defense merely patted Easie on the back.

And Penn State coach Joe Paterno, more concerned about his player's mental state than anything, came over to talk to him.

"Jimmy, look me in the eye," Paterno said. "Are you all right?"

Easie responded that he was.

"Don't worry," Paterno said. "Play your game."

So in the third period, Easie caught a touchdown pass from Tom Shuman to open a nine-point lead. Then in the fourth period, he caught another to clinch a 31-10 Penn State victory.

"I was hoping to redeem myself," Easie said.

With a little positive reinforcement, he did.

Terrific Ted

Did you know the designation of "tight end" in college football originated at Penn State? At least Penn State can claim the lion's share of the credit.

For several years the pros had featured such great tight ends as Chicago's Mike Ditka, Green Bay's Ron Kramer and Baltimore's John Mackey. But in the mid-60s pass catchers in college were all generally regarded under the generic term of "receivers."

Then big and powerful Ted Kwalick arrived at Penn State in the mid-60s, changing the look of the pass catching position that is closest to the center of the line.

Tight ends are usually used for short yardage situations. Occasionally, they will break a long run.

You couldn't tell it by Kwalick's statistics. From 1966-68 at Penn State, the big end caught 86 passes for 1,343 yards and 10 touchdowns. He became one of the first early stars at the position in college, winning All-America honors his last two years.

Kwalick was a big part of Joe Paterno's great early teams at Penn State.

"I just happened to be in the right place at the right time," Kwalick said of his contribution to college football history.

The same might be said of his pass-catching ability.

A Different Drummer

Car or piano?

Most teenagers confronted with that choice by their father would probably take the car. Not Mike Reid.

Growing up in Altoona, Pennsylvania, Reid loved music as much as he loved football. And that was a lot.

So when his father offered the high school student the choice of a used car or a piano, Reid took the musical instrument. He figured he could always walk.

Day after day, he practiced on the piano as diligently as he practiced football.

At Penn State, Reid enrolled as a music major and appeared in the play, "Guys and Dolls." He was better known as a football player—winning the Outland Trophy as the "outstanding interior lineman in college football" while keying the defense of Joe Paterno's fine teams in the late '60s.

Reid played in the NFL for five distinguished years with the Cincinnati Bengals, twice winning All-Pro before retiring. He hadn't forgotten about his other love. He wanted to see if he could make it in music.

So guess what? Turns out he was an All-Pro in that field as well.

All Reid did was go on to win many awards, including a Grammy for "Stranger in my House." He didn't stop there. He also wrote an opera.

It seemed his decision to take the piano over the car was a pretty sound one.

A Paterno Pat

Charlie Pittman had been a high school All-American. But he wasn't so confident about his college career, especially after being listed no higher than third on the Penn State freshman team depth chart.

It was spring practice in 1967 following Pittman's freshman year and he was on the varsity. Pittman continued to have serious doubts about his football career at Penn State. The tailback from Baltimore, Maryland, thought he had been buried and that no one would notice him—least of all head coach Joe Paterno.

"Here I was, this bashful inner-city kid who had never left his block, and now I was in a new environment," Pittman remembered once. "I questioned to some degree whether I belonged, whether I was good enough to be a part of this."

Paterno had to be questioning his own personal situation as well. He had taken over the Penn State football program from Rip Engle just the year before and hadn't exactly set the world on fire. His first trying year resulted in a 5-5 record.

One day Pittman walked into the locker room to find Paterno standing there.

"He sensed I was a little down," Pittman remembered. "At that time, someone—I can't remember who it was —passed us and Joe stopped him and said, 'Here's the guy who's going to make me a great football coach.'"

That certainly pumped up Pittman. But neither Pittman nor Paterno could envision the dramatic change in Penn State's football fortunes. From 1967-69 the Nittany Lions would lose only two times in 33 games, capping the 60s with two straight 11-0 seasons and No. 2 ranking in the nation both years.

And guess who was leading the way? None other than Pittman, who led the team in rushing for three straight seasons while gaining All-America status. As part of the beginning of Paterno's Penn State dynasty, Pittman set the standard for other great running backs to follow such as Lydell Mitchell, John Cappelletti, Curt Warner and D. J. Dozier.

Pittman said he owed his success to that little passing remark Paterno had made in the locker room at the end of his freshman year.

"Just that statement did so much to boost my confidence, that I turned it completely around," Pittman said.

And so did Paterno.

Special Sawbuck

What was $10 worth in 1969? Plenty, as far as the Penn State football team was concerned. To many it represented the fortunes of an entire season.

In 1968 a bamboo horseshoe was used as a good-luck charm during the Nittany Lions' perfect season. But the beloved horseshoe was stolen following Penn State's tumultuous 15-14 victory over Kansas in the Orange Bowl.

Using penny contributions from students, the Penn State cheerleaders raised enough for a crisp, new $10 bill. That would be the Nittany Lions' good luck charm to replace the ill-fated horseshoe, they decided.

The good luck bill was placed in plexiglass and chained and locked to the goal post before each game. During the week, the cheerleaders kept the bill locked in a safe. "We didn't take any chances this year," one of them said.

Each dollar stood for one of Penn State's 10 regular season games. At the end of each game, the cheerleaders asked the opposing coach to sign the bill.

The talisman was obviously working—10 games up, 10 down. Of course when Penn State faced Missouri in the Orange Bowl after an undefeated season, they needed another bill for Game 11. Back to the collection cup went the cheerleaders, who raised enough pennies for a one-dollar bill to go along with the ten.

With the two bills hanging on a goal post at the Orange Bowl, Penn State whipped Missouri 10-3 to complete an 11-0 season.

The $10 bill had indeed brought good fortune to the Nittany Lions. The only thing it couldn't buy was the No. 1 ranking in the country. Penn State finished in the second spot.

Smeared Again

It was early in the 1967 season and UCLA had just escaped with a 17-15 victory over Penn State. But for UCLA's All-America quarterback Gary Beban, it was a nightmarish outing.

Beban had spent a good part of the day on the seat of his pants, bruised and battered by Penn State's tough defense. One of his main tormentors was Steve Smear, Penn State's stalwart defensive tackle.

As he trotted to the UCLA dressing room, Beban heard someone calling his name. He turned around and, to his shock, saw Smear running toward him.

Instinctively, he broke into a run, probably fearing for his life. He had to be thinking, "Oh, no, not again."

But Smear wasn't rushing after Beban this time to deliver another crushing hit for a yardage loss. All he wanted to do was shake Beban's hand.

"I wanted to tell him that he was a great player and that he had been an idol when I was in high school and that I hoped he won the Heisman Trophy," Smear said.

It was the only time of the day that Beban didn't mind making physical contact with Smear.

Same Game, Different Season

It was 1969 and Penn State had just pulled out a thrilling comeback victory. In the locker room quarterback Chuck Burkhart had an eerie feeling, like he had been there before. In a way, he had.

The Nittany Lions' 15-14 win over Syracuse was so similar to their win over Kansas the season before in the Orange Bowl that it was positively scary. And the score was not the only reason.

Against Kansas, the Nittany Lions were playing in the Orange Bowl. Against Syracuse, they were playing against the Orange.

Like the 15-14 victory over Kansas, Penn State fell behind Syracuse early and had to make a terrific fourth-quarter comeback to pull out the game.

There were more parallels: A two-point conversion made the difference in both games. Both times, a penalty gave Penn State a second chance at the conversion after the first one failed. And it was Burkhart who called the sweep play—to Bobby Campell in the Orange Bowl and to Franco Harris at Syracuse—that gave the Nittany Lions the two conversion points they needed to win.

"To be able to turn this game around like we did has to be the greatest comeback I've ever seen," said Burkhart.

Except for another game in the Orange Bowl, of course.

Two for the Road

Sue Paterno admittedly wasn't much of a football fan when she was in high school. That soon changed, of course, when she attended Penn State and started dating Joe Paterno.

Steve Smear (number 76) was not only a great defensive player, but a class act.

Now it was the late '60s and Sue and Joe were married. She would try to make every game at home or anywhere that she could drive. She didn't let the lack of a car stop her.

One time during the 1967 season, Sue and Sandra Welsh, wife of Paterno's backfield coach George Welsh, advertised on the local radio station looking for a ride to the Navy game in Annapolis.

"As soon as I heard it on the air, I wanted to crawl into a hole, but it was too late then," Sue Paterno once recalled. "We didn't give our names, of course, but two students answered the ad."

Imagine the students' surprise when their riding companions turned out to be the wives of Joe Paterno and George Welsh.

"Boy, were they impressed when they found out who we were," Sue Paterno said. "They even bought us our lunch. Good thing, too; we only had five dollars between us."

Getting Along Swimmingly

Preparing for the 1967 Gator Bowl, the Penn State team practiced for a week under a blazing sun in Daytona Beach, Florida. It wasn't exactly ideal football weather, as far as Joe Paterno was concerned.

"The weather is great," he said, "perhaps a little too good."

In between the tiring practices under the hot Florida sun, the players managed to find some fun at their resort hotel located not far from the pounding waves of the Atlantic, to Paterno's vexation.

One morning Paterno woke up and glanced outside his window.

"There, five of my players were riding surfboards in the ocean at 7:40 a.m," Paterno said. "That woke me up real fast."

The players still proved they were in the mood for football, tying a strong Florida State team, 17-17.

One Flew Over the Football Field

When he played quarterback for Brooklyn Prep in New York in the 1940s, Joe Paterno was not especially known for his passing ability. Same thing a couple of years later at Brown University. As they used to say about Paterno as a player: all he could do was think—and win.

"Joe was never much of a passer," recalled Dick Reilly, who played in the same backfield at Brooklyn Prep with Joe and his brother, George. "He threw flutterballs."

Like many other schools of the day, Brooklyn Prep used the double-wing formation. The run, rather than the pass, was the first option. George Paterno played left halfback and Reilly, right halfback. The three became lifelong friends.

"Joe was either a running or blocking back, [there was] not much passing," Reilly recalled in a 1994 newspaper interview.

At Brooklyn Prep, Reilly remembered that Paterno "was always a straight shooter." The same couldn't be said for his ability to throw a football, however.

According to Reilly, the standing joke at Brown was that "Paterno holds the record for throwing the only end-over-end touchdown pass."

A Colorful Event

When the Nittany Lions joined the Big Ten in 1993, they were forced to discontinue many long-standing rivalries. Included were Pitt, Syracuse and West Virginia. Earlier in their history, the Lions had played some fierce battles against Army and Navy as well.

The intensity of these flaming eastern rivalries often spilled onto the Penn State campus, where the famed statue of the Nittany Lion was usually the target of troublemaking rival students.

Before Penn State, there was Brown for Joe Paterno. Here he takes a handoff from brother George.

A group of Army cadets once tried to steal the Nittany Lion, proud symbol of Penn State athletics. Penn State students had to set up guards around the statue on football weekends.

By 1966, activity around the Lion had slackened. When Syracuse came to State College that season, the statue was easy prey for some mischief makers.

They did more than paint the town. Under the cover of night, they painted the statue from nose to tail a bright, vivid orange—the predominant Syracuse school color. By morning, the freshly painted statue was the talk of a shocked Penn State campus.

The vandals were tracked down and arrested. They had to spend the weekend in jail, unable to enjoy Syracuse's 12-10 win over Penn State.

Point Made

The most important game in Joe Paterno's Penn State coaching career? It would be difficult to pick one—or even a top ten.

But you could make a case for the first time the Nittany Lions played Texas, in the 1972 Cotton Bowl.

"It was awfully important for us to beat Texas in the Cotton Bowl," Paterno said. "I felt at the time we were trying to show people what we had done in previous years was not a fluke. There was so much that had been done that was ready to go down the drain if Texas had beaten us."

The Longhorns, of course, were the team that beat out Penn State for the national championship in 1969 with Presidential blessing. Their Southwest Conference was reputed to play a better brand of football than that played in the East. Forget about Penn State's 31-game unbeaten streak and two perfect seasons in the late '60s. Detractors pointed to a "soft" eastern schedule.

Lydell Mitchell plows through a herd of Texas Longhorns in the 1972 Cotton Bowl. It was a statement game for Penn State.

Penn State halfback Lydell Mitchell, who with Franco Harris formed one of the best 1-2 backfield punches in the nation, acknowledged before the game, "Our reputation as a major football power is in question."

The Nittany Lions also needed to redeem themselves following a 31-11 loss to Tennessee that halted a 15-game winning streak and revived talk of low-quality eastern football.

Just beating the Longhorns in their own backyard would have been enough. But blowing them out? Unthinkable.

Think again. With Mitchell rushing for 146 yards, Harris throwing thunderous blocks at fullback and quarterback John Hufnagle throwing a 65-yard touchdown pass to Scott Skarzynski, the Nittany Lions wiped out the Longhorns 30-6.

In smothering Texas, Penn State held a Longhorn team without a touchdown for the first time in 80 games —or since 1964.

"I don't think we have ever had a bigger win at a time when we needed it more," Paterno said.

There wasn't as much talk about the poor quality of eastern football after that. Or at least the quality of Penn State football.

Buttle Bounces Back

Call it the "Battle of Pennsylvania" or the "Championship of Rt. 22," the bitter rivalry between Penn State and Pitt was as emotional as they come. It never mattered where either team stood in the national picture, either. One such clash took place at Three Rivers Stadium in Pittsburgh in 1974.

With an 8-2 record, Penn State had already received an invitation, if premature, to play in the Cotton Bowl. Pitt, at 7-3, was ignored by bowl selectors. The Panthers, who were on the rise under Johnny Majors, would have to make the Penn State game their bowl.

The Nittany Lions knew the Panthers would be out to make a point at their expense. Before the game, Penn State's emotional level was as high as it had been for any game that season. The Nittany Lions held a private team meeting without the coaches, trainers and doctors.

Mike Hartenstine, usually low-key, surprised his teammates with a fiery inspirational talk. Then Tom Donchez, in stronger and more emotional language, emphasized how devastating it would be to lose to Pitt. Donchez got so carried away during his pep talk that he fired his helmet against a locker.

The helmet bounced off and struck linebacker Greg Buttle between the eyes, leaving him dazed and bleeding. Later hearing of the incident, Joe Paterno grumbled, "Oh, God, can't we even get through the team prayer without an injury?"

Buttle was as tough as they come. Injured or not, he wasn't going to miss Penn State's biggest game of the year. Patched up and revved up, the linebacker took the field against the Panthers. He later reported that the first quarter seemed like a dream—everything moving in slow motion. At the half, Buttle needed six stitches for a gash over his eye. "But he never missed a signal," assistant coach Jim O'Hora reported proudly.

Nor did the Nittany Lions miss too many chances to score, whipping Pitt 31-10 with a big second-half comeback. And Buttle showed why he was an All-America player and one of a great line of linebackers at "Linebacker U."

CHAMPIONS AT LAST, AND TWO TIMES AT THAT
1980–1992

In the fast-paced age of the electronic revolution, the Nittany Lions were still doing things the old-fashioned way: a great defense and a good kicking game.

The Lions had earned the nickname "Linebacker U" with their assembly-line production of powerful linebackers and emphasis on defense. Things were no different as the world moved into the revolutionary eighties. The only thing missing at Penn State was the national championship that had eluded Joe Paterno despite a series of splendid teams in the '60s and '70s

Wait no longer. The Nittany Lions finally won the championship in 1982 and again in 1986. The Lions recouped from a three-touchdown loss to Alabama in the fifth game of the 1982 season to win the first one. SMU, the only unbeaten team in the country, finished runner-up. Penn State had been there, done that. On more than one occasion, the Lions had been denied the national title by the voters despite a perfect season.

Following the 42-21 loss to Alabama, Penn State's chances for the national title were thought by many to be finished. Penn State fullback Joel Coles thought differently. In a stirring locker room scene after the loss to Alabama, Coles told his teammates to keep the faith. "We still have six games to prove that we're a good football team," Coles said in an emotional outburst.

Paterno, who had given many stirring locker room speeches himself, didn't have to add anything.

"Joel said all that was needed to be said," Paterno told his team.

Seven victories later, including a 27-23 triumph over Georgia in the Sugar Bowl, the Nittany Lions were national champions.

Four years later, the Lions knocked off Miami 14-10 in the Fiesta Bowl to complete a 12-0 season and secure their second national title.

The Last Supper

The 1987 Fiesta Bowl between Penn State and Miami was more than just a showdown for the national championship. To many it was a morality play, a battle between good and evil: Penn State (the good guys in the white helmets) vs. Miami (the bad guys in the orange, green and white uniforms).

At least those were the public images of the football teams —squeaky-clean Penn State, which cared as much about academics as athletics, and outlaw Miami, whose graduation rate and reputation suffered·by comparison.

A series of scrapes with the law had only supported the Hurricanes' bad-boy image, which they gleefully promoted themselves. When they stepped off the plane in Arizona, the Miami players wore Rambo-style army fatigues. Even the site of their training camp seemed appropriate. It was once used by the Arizona team in the now defunct USFL. "Welcome to the Outlaws' Camp," an old banner proclaimed as they pulled in.

Before they met on the field, the Lions and Hurricanes got together for a traditional Fiesta Bowl dinner with Western-style food. It was supposed to be an evening of civility and good-natured fun with skits and presentations. It turned out to be anything but that.

After the players finished their country-fried steaks, the evening took on the tenor of a Dean Martin roast. And the Miami Hurricanes were on the spit.

First there were jokes about Vinnie Testaverde's bid for the Heisman Trophy. Not funny, thought the Hurricanes. Then other jokes with racial overtones about team unity. Even more distasteful. And finally, a shot by Penn State punter John Bruno at Miami coach Jimmy Johnson's famous meticulous hair-do.

That was when Bruno crossed the line, as far as the Miami players were concerned. At that point, Miami defensive tackle Jerome Brown angrily stood up and stormed toward the stage. He had planned to do a rap song, but suddenly decided to change his tune. He stripped off his clothes to reveal battle fatigues and spit out his feelings. "We're not here for you all to make monkeys of us, we're here to make war," he said.

He added: "Did the Japanese sit down with Pearl Harbor before they bombed them?"

Then, waving his arms to his teammates, who were all now in their fatigues, he shouted: "Let's go!" The Hurricane players followed him out of the room, a la a scene from *Animal House.*

Watching the players exit, Bruno still had one parting shot left.

"Hey, didn't the Japanese lose that one?"

As every Penn State football fan remembers, the same ending was in store for Miami in the Fiesta Bowl.

Deciphering Joe

Think Yogi Berra has a colorful way of saying things? How about Joe Paterno, whose stylized vocabulary echoes phrases from his youth in Brooklyn, N.Y.

Try these, for starters: "outta whack," "willy nilly," "loosey goosey." One local sports writer calls them "Paternoisms." Others are still not sure what they mean.

Once describing a Pitt quarterback that Penn State would face in an upcoming game, Paterno made reference to his previous performance. "Rutgers could not get him outta whack," Paterno said.

Another time while talking about Penn State tight end Brian Siverling, Paterno noted: "Brian can be as good a tight end as you'd want in college, except that every once in a while he goes down there and the ball's coming and he's very loosey goosey, just waits on it, doesn't expect to get hit."

"Willy nilly" has often come up quite often in his conversations, too.

"Willy nilly means you just don't care what happens," Paterno once explained to a reporter. "Outta whack means you're all messed up. Loosey goosey is close to willy nilly, but not the same. A loosey goosey might care, he may be interested, but if it happens it's good, and if it doesn't, that's OK."

The "Paternoisms" have rubbed off on his players. Once talking about Miami's Heisman Trophy winner Vinnie Testaverde, Penn State linebacker Shane Conlin said: "We'll have to keep him in the pocket, keep him from scrambling, because that's when he gets you outta whack."

See, even if reporters don't always understand Paterno, at least his players do.

No Bickering

It was the early 1980s and Boston College coach Jack Bicknell was making a routine recruiting visit to the home of Kevin Campbell in McLean, VA.

As he settled into a chair to begin his pitch to the highly prized high school star, Bicknell noticed that Campbell's mother was busy scurrying around the house.

"I'm in there with the kid talking, and his mother's moving around the house, dusting and cleaning," Bicknell recalled.

Bicknell soon found out why she wasn't paying any attention to him. "She's getting ready for Joe Paterno. Joe Paterno was coming to their house. Why was I there?"

Why, indeed. Paterno soon showed up after Bicknell left and Campbell was soon on his way to Penn State. It wasn't the first recruiting battle that Bicknell would lose to Paterno.

"A regular guy like me or somebody else, people are always very kind to you, but with a Paterno it's an event," Bicknell said.

Stating Their Case

For many seasons Joe Paterno had been advocating a playoff system for the national championship. And 1982 was no different.

Only this time, Penn State actually had a chance to decide the No. 1 ranking on the field. All they had to do was beat Georgia in the Sugar Bowl and they would be voted into the No. 1 spot at the end of the season for the first time.

Not finishing first in the polls had been a source of frustration and irritation at Penn State for many years.

On three previous occasions, the Nittany Lions had finished with a perfect record but were denied the No. 1 spot by the voters. In 1973 the Lions went 12-0, including a win over LSU in the Orange Bowl, yet remarkably finished only fifth in the rankings in both the AP and UPI polls.

Nevertheless, in Paterno's mind, his team was the champion after those perfect seasons in 1968, 1969 and 1973. Never mind what the voters said. But he knew that others at Penn State needed validation. "Being No. 1 is important to our fans and our kids," Paterno said.

Think how happy everyone was at Happy Valley following a 27-23 win over Georgia. There was no question which team would be voted as No. 1. After the game, Paterno faced the usual questions about a playoff system for college football.

"Next year let there be a playoff," he said. "This year, let's vote."

Jolting Joe

The Penn State-Georgia battle for No. 1 in the 1983 Sugar Bowl was a rough one—for Joe Paterno.

After Penn State's momentous 27-23 victory, the players tried to carry Paterno off the field. Good luck. They dropped him, breaking his glasses.

Undaunted, the players once again lifted Paterno to their shoulders. This time, they made it all the way across the field without dropping their precious cargo.

But by the time Paterno showed up for his postgame press conference, he looked disheveled and much the worse for wear.

He wasn't exactly in the mood to be accommodating at this point, not even when TV crews asked him to stand up from behind the microphones so he could be seen by viewers.

"What do you want me to stand for?" Paterno responded testily. "I'm tired. We played a lot of football out there."

After his wild ride across the field, Paterno had personally seen more than his share of action. Of course he remained seated.

A Nice Ring to It

After Penn State's 16-9 victory over LSU in the 1973 Orange Bowl completed a 12-0 season for the Nittany Lions, Joe Paterno didn't wait for the voters to declare the national champion. Maybe because he knew how the vote would turn out.

Holding his own "poll," he declared the Nittany Lions No 1. Then, despite Penn State's finishing fifth in both the AP and UPI polls, he went out and bought championship rings for his team and himself.

"I just felt they took it away from us in '68 and '69," Paterno said. "I wasn't going to let them take it away from us in '73."

In 1968 and 1969, Penn State failed to win the mythical national championship despite perfect seasons and bowl victories both years.

Paterno felt there was a great deal of prejudice against eastern football. Critics pointed out that Penn State played a "weak" schedule. But in that two-year stretch, the Nittany Lions were beating everyone they faced—from near and far. While playing their usual eastern rivals like Pitt, Syracuse and Navy, Penn State also took on UCLA, Colorado, Kansas State, Kansas, Missouri and Miami (Fla). And over four seasons, Penn State put together a 31-game unbeaten streak.

In 1973 "I thought we had a squad that was a great football team," Paterno said. "I thought we had one in '69 with guys like Lydell Mitchell and Franco Harris, Jack Ham, Mike Reid, those kind of people.

"Twice you can take [the national championship] away from us. The third time, I had my own poll."

So going into the battle for number one with Georgia in the 1983 Sugar Bowl, Paterno thought he had already won three national championships. Penn State fans couldn't agree more. At the Superdome in New Orleans, they hung out a banner before game time that said: "Penn State's 4th National Championship."

After the Nittany Lions beat Georgia, there was at least no argument about who was number one in the 1982 season.

Herschel Who?

It was still three nights before the 1983 Sugar Bowl, but the party was already going strong in New Orleans' French Quarter. In the streets, colors of blue (for Penn State) and red (for Georgia) dominated. Jazz drifted from the open bars while fans, high on alcohol, life and excitement, exchanged frenzied school chants.

A broad-shouldered young man strolled through the noisy streets, taking in the scene with awe like any tourist. Only this was no tourist, this was a football player looking ahead to the clash for number one between the Nittany Lions and Bulldogs.

A glint of recognition sparked in a group of assembled Georgia fans. If nothing else, this young man looked like a football player.

"Hey, what's your name?" one of them asked.

"Walker," the young man replied.

Another fan looked puzzled.

"You're not Walker," he said.

"Yes, I am. I'm Walker."

"No, you're not, you're not Herschel Walker," said the fan, referring to the great Georgia running back.

"No, I'm Walker Lee Ashley. From Penn State. You'll be hearing about me."

True to his word, Penn State's six-foot, 235-pound defensive end played heroically. Ashley was credited with five solo tackles, including three on the great Herschel Walker. On those three plays, the eventual Heisman Trophy winner gained merely a total of five yards.

After Penn State's 27-23 victory over Georgia, there was another "Walker" winning praise in college football.

Lights Out on Georgia

One day after clinching its first national championship at the 1983 Sugar Bowl, the Nittany Lions football team was back on campus soaking up all the adulation.

At a "Congratulations" rally, the coaching staff and the players who weren't in class showed up to thank their supporters.

Joe Paterno was the last to speak. He was bursting with pride, not only for his players' performance on the field but their behavior off it.

"The manager of the Hilton Hotel [where the Nittany Lions stayed in New Orleans] called and said the people at the Marriott pwhere the Georgia team stayed] had a lot of problems with the Georgia kids. There was a lot of damage. But not one single light bulb was damaged at the Hilton."

Paterno paused.

"I said that's because the Georgia kids hit harder than our kids."

Todd's Take

Penn State's first national title earned Joe Paterno, quarterback Todd Blackledge and running back Curt Warner an appearance on *Good Morning America* with host David Hartman.

Paterno revealed that the number one ranking eased some of the pressure off him and his idealistic program. Warner said his years at Penn State were "a great experience."

Then came Blackledge's turn. He was asked what his first impression of Paterno was on a practice field.

"He screamed in a high, shrill voice," Blackledge responded. "I never heard any screaming during recruiting."

Ah, but There's a Catch to It

It could be argued that Gregg Garrity's touchdown catch in the 1983 Sugar Bowl might be the most important reception in Penn State history.

Garrity made a spectacular diving catch after racing full speed into the end zone, capping a 47-yard play in the fourth quarter. It clinched a victory over Georgia and Penn State's first national football championship.

For Garrity, the hard-edged practices under Joe Paterno since being converted to wide receiver three years before had been worth it.

"When I dropped a ball in practice," Garrity said, "Joe would tell me my father only dropped one or two all season and would stay late after practice if he did. I think all the yelling paid off. I learned how to concentrate on catching the ball."

Garrity's father, Jim, was a tight end for Penn State from 1952-54. He was no easier on his son than Paterno was.

"He analyzes everything for me after the game," Gregg Garrity said of his dad. "He only tells me what I'm doing wrong."

Except for a missed pass that bounced off his shoulder pads at midfield in the first quarter, Garrity played a pretty solid game against Georgia. After Penn State's 27-23 victory, Jim Garrity complimented his son on a great game. He quickly stepped back into character, however.

"Then he brought up the one [pass] I dropped," Garrity said.

The Big Cheese

No one ever said Joe Paterno was easy to play for. That includes Joe Paterno. "Four years around me is enough, maybe too much," he once said. Like many others, Mike McCloskey felt Paterno's wrath during practice sessions.

"There were times," the tight end said in a 1983 interview, "when I wanted to scream at him. There were times I wanted to punch him out."

But also, like many others, McCloskey realized there was nothing personal in it.

"He was trying to make me better," McCloskey said. "He saw potential in me, and he wanted to squeeze out every bit of it. For my benefit, for the team's benefit, for his."

For many years, the players had a pet nickname for Paterno: "The Rat." At the team Christmas party, they gave him a present: cheese.

"He got a big kick out of it," McCloskey said. "There's no question about who's in charge, but he also encourages give and take."

One-Minute Drill

The greatest comeback in Penn State football history? Take your pick. But there haven't been too many with the significance of the Nebraska game in 1982.

The Cornhuskers were ranked No. 2 in the country when they came into Happy Valley on Sept. 25. Penn State was No. 8 after starting the season with victories over Temple, Maryland and Rutgers, not traditional national powers.

The Nittany Lions needed to beat Nebraska in this important early-season game if they were to have any chance to win the national championship. But with less than two minutes to play they trailed 24-21.

On the ensuing kickoff, an unsportsmanlike conduct penalty against Nebraska gave the Nittany Lions the ball on their 35-yard line.

Sixty-five yards to go for a touchdown and only one minute and 18 seconds left. Nervous time for the 85,304 fans crammed into Beaver Stadium. But plenty of time as far as Penn State quarterback Todd Blackledge was concerned.

"When we got the football back, I knew we had enough time to take it in," Blackledge said. "We had two timeouts and the personal foul penalty against them helped us."

Blackledge completed two passes over the middle. Quickly, Penn State was on the Nebraska 34.

But Blackledge failed to move the Lions in the next three plays. In fact, they lost ground, and now it was fourth and 11.

Blackledge had to pass. The Nittany Lions knew it. The Cornhuskers knew it. The entire stadium knew it.

Somehow, Blackledge found Kenny Jackson open for a completion, just making it past the first down marker. First and 10 on the 24-yard line.

A quarterback run and a 15-yard sideline pass to Mike McCloskey put the ball on the two. Blackledge then completed a touchdown pass to Kirk Bowman with four seconds left to lift Penn State to a dramatic 27-24 victory.

"Once we hit the fourth-and-11 pass to Kenny, I knew we would go in from there," a confident Blackledge said after the momentous victory.

How momentous? The following week the Nittany Lions lost to Alabama by 21 points and many thought that was the end of their hopes for the national title. But they won the next seven games, including a victory over Georgia in the Sugar Bowl. When the voting was completed in the national polls, Penn State finished No. 1 even though SMU was the only unbeaten team in the country.

The reason? Strength of schedule, according to the pollsters. The Nittany Lions had faced five ranked teams, and the voters put a lot of weight into their great comeback against Nebraska in the fourth game of the season.

Airily Paterno

Before the start of the 1983 Sugar Bowl game with Georgia, Joe Paterno told quarterback Todd Blackledge: "We're going to throw it and throw it and throw it. So get the arm ready."

Huh? In Paterno's earlier days as coach at Penn State, that kind of talk would have been unheard of. For many years Paterno was a conservative coach who relied largely on his defense, kicking and running game to win.

But in the 1980s, the pass became trendy, in large measure thanks to Blackledge's terrific arm. While it wasn't exactly "Air Paterno," it was a far cry from the old image of "Linebacker U" at Penn State.

Blackledge had a flair for dramatic performances. In 1982 he led the Nittany Lions to comeback wins over Maryland, Nebraska, Notre Dame, Boston College and Pittsburgh. And

Blackledge's touchdown pass in the fourth quarter secured Penn State's 27-23 Sugar Bowl win over Georgia.

A couple of weeks later, at a luncheon honoring the Lions, Paterno acknowledged—tongue in cheek—that he was adjusting his football philosophy.

"You sure make us want to do it [win a national title] again," he told the audience. "And now that we know how to throw a pass, we might do it again."

Heisman, Shmeisman

Getting ready for the 1983 Sugar Bowl against Georgia, Penn State was obviously focused on Heisman Trophy winner Herschel Walker.

In the days leading up to the big game in New Orleans, the Nittany Lions put together an elaborate defensive scheme for Walker that included stunting and gang tackling. In practices, the Nittany Lions simulated game conditions by having big backs the size of Walker run at the defense.

Still, Joe Paterno was not so sure any of it would work against the real Herschel Walker. Asked what kind of a plan he had in mind for stopping the great Georgia runner, Paterno quipped: "I've got a guy coming in from Canada to make him an offer he can't refuse."

Actually, the Lions didn't need any help from outside. They held Walker to 103 yards on 28 carries, far below his average.

Meanwhile, it was the Georgia Bulldogs who should have been worried about Penn State's Curt Warner. For the second straight year, he outplayed a Heisman Trophy winner with 117 yards on 18 carries as Penn State beat Georgia. The year before, Warner did the same against Southern Cal's Marcus Allen as the Nittany Lions won the Fiesta Bowl.

A Nice Retirement Gift

Penn State president Dr. John Oswald had already announced his retirement date before Penn State faced Georgia in the 1983 Sugar Bowl.

Oswald, due to retire in June, told Joe Paterno he had his retirement present already picked out: a national championship.

While Oswald had put in his request to Paterno, the Penn State coach wasn't promising anything. But he would certainly try.

"Joe told me he recognized I was a 'senior,' and he was going to miss me next year," Oswald said. "but that he was going to miss [senior tailback] Curt Warner even more."

Warner went on to deliver in the Sugar Bowl and Paterno delivered the national championship "present" to Oswald.

Not So Sweet

The "Super Bowl of College Football." The "Bowl of Champions." The "Sugar Bowl Shootout."

The 1983 Sugar Bowl was really hyped by television and newspapers. Oh, boy, was it hyped. After all, it wasn't often that the nation's No. 1 and No. 2 teams met for the national championship. It had happened only five times before on New Year's Day.

Before the game Paterno warned his players not to get caught up in the drum beating. "Forget about the garbage," he told his team.

Dan Biondi, a walk-on who became an important part of the Nittany Lions' defensive backfield, related one of Paterno's well-known aphorisms.

"Joe always says publicity is like poison," Biondi said. "It won't hurt you unless you swallow it."

Pigskin and Proverbs

On the eve of the 1983 Sugar Bowl between Penn State and Georgia, *The Times Picayune* of New Orleans conducted a poll of reporters. The question: Who is going to win the game, and why?

Many of the reporters answered the question with sobering seriousness. Others, like Gordon White of the *New York Times*, took the lighthearted approach.

In picking undefeated Georgia to beat once-beaten Penn State, White relied on an "old Chinese proverb. Never go against a winner until the winner becomes a loser."

A few others also had capricious comments. Malcolm Moran, also covering for the *New York Times*, made reference to Penn State's last appearance in the Sugar Bowl. That one ended in a 14-7 loss to Alabama when Penn State was unable to run the ball over from the one-yard line. The Nittany Lions' inability to score from 12 inches out cost them the national championship.

"This time, if they face a fourth down on the goal line," they'll throw," said Moran in picking Penn State.

Pat Livingstone of the *Pittsburgh Press* made reference to Dean Smith's first national basketball championship at North Carolina: "Law of averages will finally dictate that Joe Paterno finally wins his first national championship—keeping up with the Smiths."

Mike Littwin of the *Los Angeles Times* picked Penn State with the cavalier rejoinder: "Why not?"

The Times-Picayune's—the *States Item's* own Dave Lagarde wasn't even in the same ballpark when asked about the winner. His response: "Saints 34, Falcons 3. Oops! That one's on Sunday."

Making a Statement

Any college football team seeking the national championship usually has a "statement" game or two at some point of the season.

For Penn State in 1986, that important moment came when the Nittany Lions traveled to Alabama for a battle of unbeaten teams. The Crimson Tide was ranked No. 2 in the country, while Penn State was No. 6.

But not a legitimate No. 6. At least that was the general opinion of sports writers, who thought Penn State had played a soft schedule through its first six games. And the Nittany Lions had almost lost to underdog Cincinnati at that, pulling out the game with a late touchdown.

Alabama, meanwhile, had beaten the likes of Ohio State and Tennessee, the latter by a big score. And the Crimson Tide had a 13-game unbeaten streak, best in the nation.

Talk about a team having to prove a point. A Penn State victory over Alabama, no matter how close, would certainly do it.

Good luck. That's what many of the media thought—many of them covering the game were prepared to write Penn State's obituary, just as they had in losses at Alabama in 1982 and 1984.

Imagine their surprise when Penn State, a six-point underdog, beat Alabama decisively, 23-3. No contest. All thanks to the Nittany Lions' best defensive performance of the season.

"The most vivid memory of that game is how Penn State stopped us on first down," said Alabama line coach Jim Fuller. "They just took first down away from us."

It had to go down as one of the most satisfying triumphs in Penn State football history. By now, Penn State's "soft" schedule had been forgotten.

And it was completely dismissed after the Nittany Lions capped a 12-0 season with a win over Miami (Fla.) in the Fiesta Bowl for their second national championship. It was statement game number two for that season.

Undaunted Blair

Despite an amazing high school career in Philadelphia, Blair Thomas knew he wasn't going to play much in his first two years at Penn State. Not with seniors D. J. Dozier and Dave Clark at the tailback position.

He did pick his spots, though, in his sophomore season of 1986. And in an odd coincidence, the same number kept coming up each time Thomas broke out.

In one game, he ripped off a 92-yard run from scrimmage against Syracuse to smash a 92-year-old school record. Then he dashed 92 yards with a kickoff return against Pitt.

These bursts of brilliance sent a signal to Joe Paterno that Thomas would be ready to start as a junior. Thomas had no doubt.

"I've used my two years as a learning experience," he said. "Hopefully, I can get out there and contribute."

Talk about an understatement. Thomas became the first running back in Penn State history to gain 1,300 or more yards for two seasons.

There was more to Thomas's story than just that. After a brilliant junior season, he sat out a year recuperating from reconstructive knee surgery. All he did was come back in his senior year and rush for eight 100-yard games and 1,341 yards.

Thomas finished his Penn State career with 4,512 all-purpose yards, including 3,301 rushing. He was selected for the All-American team and finished in the top ten in the Heisman Trophy voting.

Not bad for a player who spent two years mainly sitting on the bench, and then overcoming the most serious surgery for a running back.

A Dirty Job, But...

A romantic might call them the engine room of the offense. But in the real world, they live in anonymity with only bumps and bruises to show for their blocks. No one ever notices them—unless they're run over by the opposition's defense. Really, who would want to be an offensive lineman?

Chris Conlin, for one.

"You probably have to be a little sick in the mind," said Penn State's All-America tackle of the '80s.

As a college player, Conlin idolized Conrad Dobler, the onetime all-pro guard with the St. Louis Cardinals. Dobler was known as "Dracula in cleats" for his dirty play. Dobler admitted actually biting opposing players.

"He was saying you have to be dirty, that you have to bite, kick, hold, scratch, do anything you have to do to get the job done," Conlin said after watching a show about Dobler on *ESPN*. "And that's pretty much the way it is."

While starting three years, Conlin was one of the most versatile football players ever at Penn State.

In 1983 as a freshman, he played both guard and tackle during the regular season. In the Aloha Bowl against Washington, he switched to defensive tackle.

When he became a full-time starter as a sophomore, he anchored the offensive line at tackle and soon established himself as one of the nation's top linemen. He was a key player for the Nittany Lions as they drove for the national championship in 1986.

"It's true that offensive linemen get the least notice," Conlin said in an interview during the 1986 season. "It's like

Blair Thomas's sophomore season was only a sign of great things to come.

we could run for 450 yards [blocking for backs] and you hear nothing about us. Sometimes you get ticked off about it. But the other guys on the team and the coaches notice us."

A Major Decision

As a running back, D. J. Dozier was pretty decisive about where he was going. The same couldn't be said about his choice of a major at Penn State.

In four years, Dozier changed his major at least four or five times. He started with business, then went to hotel restaurant management, and moved on to marketing before going back to business.

Was he all set then? Not on your life. He ultimately landed in tourism, thinking about possibly working for an airline or as a travel agent after football.

One career he hadn't thought about was administration of justice. But the 1986 Penn State yearbook did, listing that as his major. It puzzled Dozier, to say nothing of his family.

"I don't know why they put that in there," Dozier said in a 1986 interview. "My dad thought I'd changed my major again."

Dozier ultimately wound up as a minister in Centre Hall, Pa.

A Classy Program

When he first took over the Penn State football program in 1966, Joe Paterno raised a lot of eyebrows and inspired some skepticism with his so-called "Grand Experiment." The idea of winning with athletes who were also good students seemed foreign to many big-time college coaches.

Well, after so many years it can't be called an "experiment" anymore. Pay attention, now class. Everyone knows

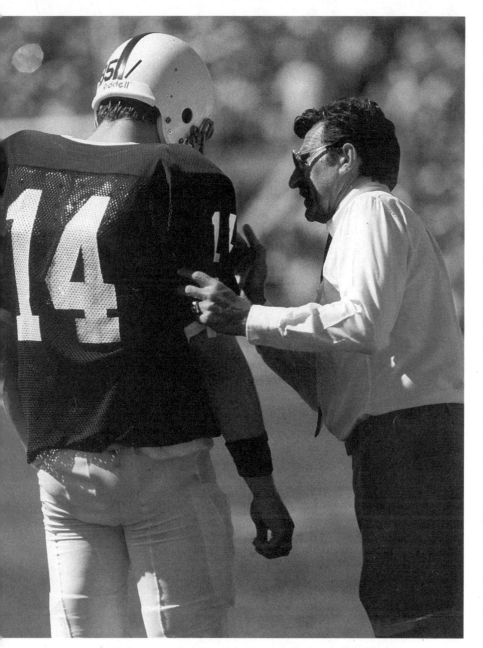

Joe Paterno makes his point to quarterback John Shaffer.

about Paterno's great winning percentage (82 percent going into the 2003 season). Turns out, the graduation rate of the football team has been even higher (85 percent, according to the university).

During the 1986 season, Penn State quarterback John Shaffer, a finance major with a 3.2 grade point average, was very direct about the sincerity of the "Grand Experiment."

"People are always asking me if the academic stuff is true or if it's all hype," Shaffer said. "Let me tell you, it's all true. You're better off missing a tackle than missing class. Coach'll kill you if you miss class."

Simply Perfect

The 1986 season marked the 100th year of Penn State football, and coach Joe Paterno made sure his team knew it.

"He tells us there've been 100 teams through here and we don't want to be just another one of the crowd," quarterback John Shaffer said in an interview during that season.

Although Paterno insisted he didn't want a national championship for himself, "naturally I'd like to see us get it for the kids. They had a shot at it last year and I'd like to see them win."

Paterno referred to the 1986 Orange Bowl, when Penn State had a perfect season spoiled by Oklahoma.

Just like a pitcher going for a no-hitter in baseball, Paterno seemingly didn't like to talk about a national championship with his players during the 1986 season.

"I'll needle 'em once in a while," Paterno said in an interview. "'You don't look like national champions to me.' That's about all."

That season, the Nittany Lions had the chance to be the first Penn State team to win the national championship with a perfect record. The 1982 team won the school's first championship with one loss.

"That's definitely on our minds," Shaffer said.

Whether it was the players' self-motivation, Paterno's prodding or just a matter of fate, the stars were aligned for the Nittany Lions in 1986. In their 100th season, they finished with a 12-0 record and the national championship after beating Miami in the Fiesta Bowl.

Talk about everything fitting together just perfectly— a rarity in this world. It was a nice way to complete a century of football at Penn State.

One More Time

Winning his first national championship was more satisfying than Joe Paterno ever imagined. And not for the obvious reason that it ended years of frustration at Penn State.

"I didn't feel any different [after the 27-23 victory over Georgia in the 1983 Sugar Bowl], "Paterno said. "But when we flew back to Harrisburg two days later, the streets were lined with people for 90 miles.

"It was the most moving sight I've ever had. I thought to myself, 'This is super. Let's do it again.'"

And so Penn State did, in 1986. The reception was no less enjoyable for Paterno then, either.

Nittany Lions, Meet the Gipper

In 1987 President Reagan obviously had a lot on his mind —he was recovering from prostate surgery and was beleaguered by questions about the Iran-Contra arms deal.

Still, he took time out to honor the Penn State football team at the White House after the Nittany Lions beat Miami for the national championship in the Fiesta Bowl.

Reagan knew his way around sports. He had played football at Eureka College (Ill.) and had played the role of Notre Dame football legend George Gipp in the 1940 movie, *Knute Rockne, All-American*.

But as a rookie sportscaster on WOC radio in Davenport, Iowa, he didn't know as much as he thought about college football.

"In one broadcast I referred to the Nittany Lions, and I got letters from all over because I was talking to the *Columbia* Lions, and I found out who the Nittany Lions really were," Reagan remembered.

In 1987 he could not forget them, following their pulsating 14-10 victory over the Hurricanes that included a tremendous goal-line stand at the end.

Reagan, who was given a Nittany Lions cap and shirt and a miniature Nittany Lions statue, said he was inspired by that goal-line stand.

"Next time I go see Congress, I might just wear that Nittany Lions hat," he said.

All-American Wife

Throughout his successful coaching career, Joe Paterno has many times given the lion's share of credit to his wife, Sue.

Citing her strength in many roles as wife, mother, homemaker, hostess, student adviser and cheerleader, Paterno never forgets to bring up her name at public rallies or in speeches.

Paterno, nicknamed "JoePa" by his fans, was at such a parade and rally at State College honoring the Nittany Lions' 1986 national championship team.

Taking the mike before a crowd estimated from 25,000 to 35,000, Paterno introduced his staff one by one—each of them getting a roar.

Introducing his better half got a little different reaction. "This is SuePa," he said, evoking chuckles from the large crowd.

Unconventional

Not long after Penn State beat Miami in the 1987 Fiesta Bowl for the national championship, Joe Paterno addressed a football coaches convention in San Diego, California.

Some 1,000 mostly young coaches listened enthralled while Paterno told them of his fond memories of such conventions.

The first time he attended a coaching clinic, he was in his mid-20s, a first-year assistant under Rip Engle at Penn State.

"Four of us got in a car and drove all night from State College to Dallas," Paterno remembered. "The University gave us 50 bucks apiece for expenses."

It was late at night when the four exhausted travelers arrived in Dallas. Paterno was ready to go to sleep—or thought he was until he saw a big crowd in the lobby "surrounding this kind of heavy guy holding court."

The "heavy guy" was Woody Hayes, who had just finished an unbeaten season at Miami of Ohio and was on his way to greatness at Ohio State. Suddenly, Paterno and his buddies weren't tired anymore. They stuck around listening to Hayes "until about 4 o'clock in the morning."

Paterno said he picked up a lot of pearls of wisdom at these conventions. Once attending a coaching clinic in St. Louis, Paterno shared an elevator with none other than Notre Dame coach Frank Leahy, Oklahoma's Bud Wilkinson and Georgia's Wally Butts. Paterno was just a face in the crowd then.

One of the coaches pressed the button for the eighth floor. Paterno was supposed to get off on the third, but went along for the ride to eavesdrop on their conversation. He hoped to pick up some information on coaching football, and wasn't disappointed.

"I was damned if I was going to get off on the third floor," Paterno recalled. "I went right up there with them."

Wired

Penn State had just won the 1987 Fiesta Bowl in Tempe, Arizona, and Joe Paterno was basking in the glow of the victory over Miami that gave the Nittany Lions their second national championship.

An Associated Press reporter at the postgame news conference, meanwhile, was looking ahead instead of looking behind.

Veteran wire service man Ralph Bernstein had heard enough about the game. He needed fresh information for follow-up stories to fill a couple of cycles on the AP wire.

"What about the future of Penn State football, given the team's unusually large graduating class?" Bernstein asked Paterno.

The Penn State coach chuckled.

"Hey, Bernstein, what are you looking for, another trip?" Paterno said.

Paterno added another crack.

"Give me at least one day to enjoy this baby. I love you, Ralph, but talk to me a month from now."

Turns out, Paterno didn't even have a day to enjoy one of his greatest triumphs. Less than 24 hours later, he was on the phone chatting with possible recruits for the 1987 season. Winning the national championship didn't make it any easier to recruit, either.

"It's a constant battle," Paterno said. "Now, instead of guys telling recruits you're no good, they're telling 'em we're loaded. You can't win."

A Gift for Penn State

The 1987 Fiesta Bowl was a match made in football heaven—the nation's No. 1 team (Miami) against No. 2 (Penn State).

The game lived up to the hype. With a little over two minutes to play, the Hurricanes were fourth-and-six on their own 27-yard line trailing 14-10. Miami coach Jimmy Johnson decided to go for it.

Bingo! First down, on a 31-yard pass play from Heisman Trophy winner Vinnie Testaverde to Brian Blades.

"I was worried," Penn State coach Joe Paterno said. "In my experience, whenever I've taken a big, big gamble like that, I've usually won. The kids get to thinking, 'Look out, this must be our night.' And everything starts to happen. I was scared."

It got scarier. With Testaverde passing right and left, Miami marched downfield. All of a sudden, the Hurricanes had second-and-goal on the Penn State five with 48 seconds left. The team with the nation's best offense had three tries to go only five yards for the game-winning touchdown.

Testaverde went back to pass, but was sacked by tackle Tim Johnson.

Third and goal on the 13.

Testaverde tried another pass. Incomplete.

Fourth and goal on the 13, with 18 seconds left.

One play for the national championship.

Once again, Testaverde put the ball in the air. This time, Penn State linebacker Pete (Gifto) Giftopoulos intercepted.

The Penn State fans went wild as their team held on for the victory. Holding onto the ball was another thing for Giftopoulos. He quickly handed it to an official after his big play. Actually, the reason had a practical application.

"Why should I keep it?" said Giftopoulos, of Hamilton, Ontario. "If you keep it you've got to give the NCAA $50. That's $75 Canadian."

On the Attack

After the 1987 Fiesta Bowl game, backup quarterback Matt Knizer was late getting on the Penn State team bus.

"Here's our leader and he's late," Joe Paterno said of the player who would probably be the starting quarterback for the 1987 season.

Knizer didn't apologize for making everyone wait. Instead he went on the offense. He shot a glance at John Shaffer, the senior who finished a fine career with the 14-10 victory over Miami. Shaffer had been 27-1 as a starter at Penn State.

"Yeah," Knizer cracked, "you're a has-been, Shaffer."

Mellowing?

Joe Paterno's hot and cold relationship with sports writers has been well documented through the years. So some had a warm and fuzzy feeling when the Penn State coach issued a heartfelt thanks to reporters after the 1987 Fiesta Bowl for following team interview procedures.

After all, Paterno had been sharp with the press on other occasions. One of his much publicized remarks:

"If I ever need a brain transplant, I want one from a sports writer. That way, I'll know it's never been used."

At the time he was thanking the media, Paterno probably wasn't aware that a power failure in a part of Sun Devils

Stadium had caused a delay in the statistics usually handed out in the press box. More than 900 media members, many of them on tight deadlines for the night game, had to wait until well into the third period before getting the halftime stats.

There was no word whether any of them blamed Paterno for that delay.

Heisman Who?

It was halftime at the 1987 Fiesta Bowl and a couple of famous alumni were being interviewed on TV about the Penn State-Miami game.

One was Jim Kelly, the former University of Miami star then with the Buffalo Bills. The other was Curt Warner, who had played at Penn State before going on to the pros with the Seattle Seahawks.

Predictably, Kelly said he hoped that Miami's Heisman Trophy-winning quarterback Vinnie Testaverde "does what Bernie Kosar and I have done so far." Kosar, also a former Miami star, had made it in the pros with the Cleveland Browns.

Warner, quite naturally, said he thought his former team had a good chance to beat Miami. The teams were tied 7-7 at the half.

"No one is going to blow out Penn State," he said. "They have a long history of stopping Heisman Trophy winners."

Indeed. In the 1982 Fiesta Bowl, the Nittany Lions had put a blanket on Southern Cal's Marcus Allen to beat the Trojans, 26-10. And in the 1983 Sugar Bowl, they had held Herschel Walker to a subpar game while beating Georgia, 27-23.

So, true to form, the Nittany Lions tormented Testaverde. They intercepted five of his passes, causing him to play the worst game of his college career. Testaverde had been intercepted only nine times for the entire 1986 season.

And, of course, another Heisman Trophy winner bit the dust as the Nittany Lions knocked off Miami, 14-10, for the national championship.

Warner was right on the money, if Testaverde wasn't.

Signing Up

It was a Fiesta Bowl matchup between No. 1 and No. 2 and naturally, the creative sign makers came out in full force in Sun Devils Stadium for national television.

"Brothers In Arms," said one sign, referring to Miami's receiver Brian Blades and his brother, free safety Bennie Blades.

"Shane—Pains for Canes," said another, referring to Penn State linebacker Shane Conlan.

Another sign, though, had nothing to do with football. But it did have a more immediate message. It was from a Penn State fan, whose banner read:

"Bobby Theys! Yes, I'd love to marry you!"

Father Doesn't Always Know Best

Shane Conlan thought he was making the right decision. His father wasn't so sure.

Conlan's father, a state policeman in Frewburg, N.Y., hoped his son would turn pro after he finished his fourth year at Penn State. But Conlan, who had a year of eligibility left, wanted to come back for that final year. He was looking for redemption, following Penn State's 25-10 loss to Oklahoma in the 1986 Orange Bowl that cost the Nittany Lions the national championship.

But what if he injured himself during the 1986 season? How would that impact his pro career? That was what his father worried about. So before the season, he took out an insurance policy on his son.

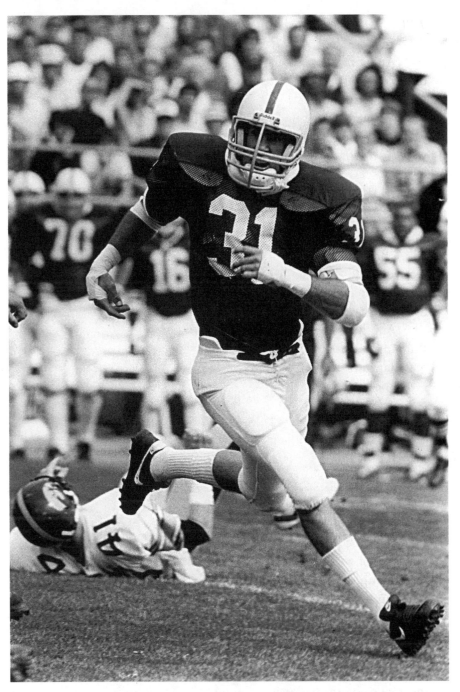

Shane Conlan: Glad he didn't listen to his father

Game in, game out, Conlan keyed Penn State's tough defense from his linebacker position. And Penn State kept winning. The Nittany Lions finished the regular season with an 11-0 record and found themselves in the Fiesta Bowl, with another chance to win the national championship.

In the first quarter, Conlan was forced to the sidelines with a knee injury. You couldn't blame his father if he had any thoughts, however fleeting, of a career-ending injury.

However, Conlan returned to the game and played a key role—making two interceptions and eight tackles despite a pained knee and sheer exhaustion. His second interception in the fourth quarter set up Penn State's go-ahead touchdown against Miami.

"My knee bothered me, but I said they'd have to drag me off the field, because I wasn't going," Conlan said. "If I lost my leg then, I would have hopped off."

The Nittany Lions held on for the victory, capping what Conlan called a "perfect career."

It was one time that his father was probably glad his son didn't listen to him.

Low Cost, High Yield

While at Penn State from 1983-86, quarterback John Shaffer went about his work unspectacularly. He was not considered a great passer, or a great runner. His personal statistics rarely stuck out. However, the yields were great.

One of the rare times he lost—in fact, the only time—came in the 1986 Orange Bowl. Penn State was beaten 25-10 by Oklahoma, costing the Nittany Lions the national championship. Shaffer was maligned after that defeat, but he worked hard for a chance at redemption.

That came against Miami in the 1987 Fiesta Bowl, another game for the national championship. Shaffer's stats again weren't exactly sparkling—he only completed five of 16 passes for 53 yards with one interception. But Shaffer scored a touchdown and the Nittany Lions won, 14-10, to finish a 12-0 season.

It also finished an extraordinary bull run for Shaffer in football. Dating back to the seventh grade, he had won 66 of 67 games as a starter.

After making more gains than losses in football, Shaffer went to work in the stock market. His field of expertise? Why, high-yield bonds, of course.

JoePa's Slight Misjudgment

Joe Paterno doesn't mind admitting he made a mistake in judging talent. In one instance it took him several years to do it, though.

In trying to recruit one particular quarterback from East Brady, Pennsylvania, Paterno told him he would like to use him as a linebacker. Not for this kid, even though that was a high-profile position at Penn State. He headed to the University of Miami, where quarterbacks were king.

Jim Kelly became one of the most famous and successful quarterbacks in pro football while playing for the Buffalo Bills.

At the 1987 Fiesta Bowl, Kelly came back to support his alma mater in the national championship game against Penn State. He ran into Paterno at a hotel in Scottsdale, Arizona.

"A fine linebacker you turned out to be," Paterno quipped.

In Love with Both

For an expert evaluation of the teams in the 1987 Fiesta Bowl, you couldn't find a better source than Cincinnati coach Dave Currey.

His team had played both Penn State and Miami. The Bearcats lost to the Hurricanes, 45-13, and to the Nittany Lions, 23-17.

Currey said it was a close call between the teams.

"They're both great—one you'd date and the other you'd marry," he noted.

He didn't say which was which, although Penn State did wind up wearing the ring.

Paterno's Pitch

The uniforms are described as "plain vanilla," the campus is isolated and the cultural life is nothing to write home about.

Rogers Alexander, a Penn State linebacker from 1982-85, described State College as "a place in the middle of the sticks with one night club and 40 local hangout bars that you can do all within a week without a car." Pete Kugler, a defensive lineman for the Nittany Lions from 1979-80, called Penn State "probably the most unattractive school I visited."

Yet Penn State year after year continues to lure some of the nation's top football talent. How does Joe Paterno do it?

"Joe, more than anything, plays on your parents," said Kugler. "He almost ignores the kid."

It's generally known that Paterno sells the prospective player, as well as the parents, on the strong academic environment at Penn State. Oh, yes, the football tradition might also enter into the conversation at some point.

Mark Robinson, who became an investment advisor after his college and pro football career were over, summed up Paterno's pitch for recruits about as well as anyone.

Robinson said Paterno showed his "parents study hall instead of the cheerleaders."

The Robinsons were sold.

Say Hello to Joe

It figures. You can't go anywhere on Penn State's campus (or adjoining College Avenue, for that matter) without running into some kind of memorabilia featuring Joe Paterno. The Penn State coach is even featured in an irreverent comic campus handbook, "Are You a Penn Stater?"

As expressed in the book, one of the requirements for the true Penn Stater is to "drink from a keg on an apartment balcony." Another: "To see a porno flick on campus."

Those would both be topped by the real essence of the Penn State experience, though: "Say 'Hi!' to Joe Paterno."

"It's usually a great thrill to say 'Hi!' when you see JoePa walking across campus—especially when you see him for the first time," the book says. "At least it's something you can tell Mom and Dad about during your next phone call home."

Then, of course, the student could talk about grades.

Halo, Joe

Like many other high profile figures, Joe Paterno is a target for both praise and pans. Other football coaches don't mind taking a jab at Joe once in a while. This was certainly the case when Paterno, voted Sportsman of the Year in 1986 by *Sports Illustrated*, brought his Penn State team to Phoenix for the Fiesta Bowl.

Before the game, Miami coach Jimmy Johnson was asked if it wouldn't be a good idea to play a tiebreaker, if needed.

Knowing that the NCAA was dead set against any such thing, he said tongue in cheek: "If Miami put in a petition, I don't think it would have the clout that it would if St. Joe did it. After all, he's the Sportsman of the Year."

Johnson was making reference to Paterno's squeaky clean image as a football coach.

It was not anything that Paterno hadn't heard before. And he appeared to take Johnson's remark in the playful spirit of the moment.

Later meeting the media himself, Paterno quipped:

"I left my halo at the house."

No Joke

With a conservative offense that featured a strong running attack, Penn State was highly successful—if sometimes predictable—during the 1986 season.

So the popular "Joe Paterno" golf balls featuring the coach's face that were sold at State College spawned a long-standing campus joke:

Like Paterno's offense, three out of four golf balls are guaranteed to go straight up the middle.

Friendly Enemies

For six hours they were seat companions on a flight from New York to Los Angeles, just two college football players exchanging pleasant conversation.

Well, maybe not just *any two* college football players. One was Penn State linebacker Shane Conlan. The other, Miami quarterback Vinnie Testaverde. They were on their way to California to tape Bob Hope's Christmas TV special honoring the Kodak All-Americans.

Although both knew they would be mortal enemies on the field in the 1987 Fiesta Bowl, for now they were just a couple of guys enjoying each other's company.

Conlan and Testaverde had gravitated toward each other at previous functions and found they had a lot in common personality-wise. Both were quiet and unassuming and had a distaste for self-promotion. The more they talked, the more they found a special bond.

Of course discussion of the Fiesta Bowl came up during the flight. It would be the last college game for either player, one final chance at the national championship. For both, a chance at redemption after losing previous national championship games.

"He asked me what we were going to do [defensively] and I said, 'Aw, I don't know,'" Conlan said with a laugh. "It was no big deal talking about the game. He's such a good guy. On the field, I'll hate him and I'm sure he'll hate me. But there won't be anything cheap."

When the game started, the friendship went on the back burner. Conlan was at his ferocious best, making eight tackles and two interceptions of Testaverde's passes. His second pickoff in the fourth quarter set up Penn State's winning touchdown in a 14-10 victory.

With friends like Conlan, Testaverde didn't need any enemies, it turned out. At least on the football field. .

Winning Ugly

Penn State's football uniforms are nothing to write home about. That's the way they're supposed to be — "plain vanilla," as they say.

No stars, bars or skulls on the helmet signifying individual achievement, just white with a blue stripe down the middle. And the jerseys, usually basic blue at home and white on the road. And certainly no names on the back. If Joe Paterno could get away with it, there probably wouldn't be any numbers, either.

It's part of Paterno's philosophy emphasizing the team, losing yourself to a cause bigger than the individual.

Like many other players, Penn State safety Ray Isom "hated" the no-frills uniform at first. "But it doesn't take long before you realize it's what's inside that counts," he said. "The rest is nothing but window dressing."

Penn State even disdained patches signifying a special event such as a bowl game. Isom recalled a scene before the 1986 Orange Bowl against Oklahoma. By then, the Penn State players had been brainwashed against any garish addition to their uniform.

"Joe held up these little miniature oranges next to a jersey so we'd have an idea what they'd look like. Then, one by one, you'd hear guys saying, 'Nah. Forget it. Too gaudy. Wouldn't look right on us.'"

As expected, "plain vanilla" won out in the end.

A Scary Time

Nothing came easy for the Nittany Lions during the 1987 season. And when things were going bad, Penn State quarterback Matt Knizner usually took the brunt of the fans' displeasure.

On October 30, the Lions were seemingly on their way to a loss to West Virginia at State College. The Mountainers led 21-10 with less than 10 minutes to go.

When Knizner took the field, he was showered with boos. His game had been flat, particularly in the third period when he threw three passes—two incomplete and one intercepted, which led to a West Virginia touchdown.

No matter. He quickly and calmly engineered a touchdown drive in one minute, 48 seconds. Then after the Lions got the ball on their own 38 with 5:43 to go, Knizner led them on another TD drive for a 25-21 victory. It was one of the greatest comebacks in Joe Paterno's career to that point.

By the end of the game, the fans boos had turned to cheers for Knizner. Not that he seemed to notice.

After the game, Penn State offensive guard Steve Wisniewski was upset about the fans' fickle display. He asked Knizner what it felt like to be booed in his own stadium.

Not missing a beat, the cool Knizner responded: "Oh, were they booing me? I thought they were booing because of Halloween."

A Real Standout

While playing for Penn State from 1984-87, Trey Bauer stood out—and not just because of his great success at the linebacker position. Bauer was never afraid of a challenge or to speak his mind, no matter the circumstances. At times his nonconformist behavior stretched the patience of the Penn State coaching staff to the limit.

Early in his career at Penn State, Bauer constantly fought with teammates. Recalled Trey's father, Charlie Bauer, who coached him at Paramus (N.J.) High School: "Joe Paterno and [assistant coach] Fran Gantner came to me and said, 'We know how tough Trey is. He doesn't have to fight with his teammates to prove it.' Twice they told me that."

Paterno had no choice but to let Bauer channel his aggression to the football field. He made him a starter sooner rather than later.

He became an exceptional linebacker, teaming with Shane Conlan as a devastating one-two defensive punch on Penn State's national champions of 1986. Bauer's behavior still bordered on the edge. When defensive coordinator Jerry Sandusky prodded him one day during a spring practice, Bauer gave just as much back. Some felt he was being disrespectful.

Then there was the 1987 Fiesta Bowl game with Miami. When the Hurricanes' Jerome Brown said Penn State ran a "racist" program, Bauer's reaction juiced up the story for the newspapers even more. "That shows what kind of intellect he has," Bauer said.

When the Miami players tried to unnerve the Nittany Lions by running through their pre-game drills, a football came whistling dangerously close to a Miami player's helmet. It was Bauer who had thrown it, naturally.

Bauer already had a degree in Speech Communications by the spring of 1987. He was still eligible for another year of football, but could have skipped it for the NFL. He came back to play one more year at Penn State.

Paterno, asked if he had talked Bauer into returning for a fifth year, responded with a laugh:

"You don't talk to Trey. You listen to him. He just told me, 'You're going to have to put up with me for another year.'"

There Was No Answer for It

When Blair Thomas played tailback for Penn State in the 1980s, few players were ever respected—or liked—more. Known as a great player, Thomas was also regarded as a good person. He didn't like to turn down an autograph request and usually hung around and talked to tailgaters after games at Beaver Stadium.

Now it was the 1989 season and Thomas was making his return from a year off because of knee surgery. During an interview, Thomas was asked an unusual question: Name something bad about himself, something he's embarrassed about.

He had a hard time coming up with an answer. Squirming in his chair, Thomas said after a while, "I can't think of anything now."

He paused. But wait, he just remembered something.

"Sometimes I consider myself shy," he said. "There's a lot of things I wouldn't do or say. And my girlfriend thinks I'm a little too nice. I go out of my way to do things for people."

Thomas leaned back in his chair and reconsidered his response.

"That's not something really bad, though," he said thoughtfully.

Thomas paused for a while longer, a puzzled look on his face.

"I'm gonna have to get back to you on this one," he said finally.

Up Close and Personal

When Penn State had its first losing season in over half a century in 1988, the shockwaves could be felt all over State College. No one was more troubled than Joe Paterno, who blamed himself for the 5-6 year. He felt he had distanced himself too much from his team and lost touch with his players.

"I've got to spend more time with these kids," he said, "and get to know which of them are the right kind of people."

He promised things would change. He would go back to being more of a hands-on coach, mixing with his players just like the old days. "I don't know if it was a promise or a threat," he said. "It depends upon who you're talking to."

Joking aside, Penn State went 8-3-1 the following season and beat Brigham Young in the Holiday Bowl. Paterno's personal touch had apparently made some difference.

Looking Rosy

It was 1992, one year before Penn State started its Big Ten football schedule. Penn State athletic director Jim Tarman happened to be in California for a speaking engagement directly across the street from the Rose Bowl.

Tarman had never been inside the famed arena, so he asked a security guard if he could inspect the place.

"No way," the guard said.

"But you don't understand," Tarman said. "I'm from Penn State, and I have to get in. You see, we are going to play in the Rose Bowl on January 1, 1994."

The guard not only let Tarman in, but ended up giving him a guided tour. As it turned out, Tarman's optimism was well founded. Penn State did play in the Rose Bowl, only it was a year later. The Nittany Lions beat Oregon 38-20 on January 2, 1995 to cap a perfect 12-0 season in only their second year in the Big Ten.

A Big Splash in the Big Ten
1993–Present

In an era that featured the rise of the stock market and the fall of the Soviet Union, Penn State football also had its share of gains and losses.

The Nittany Lions joined the Big Ten, now a misnomer with 11 teams. At the same time, they lost relations with many of their traditional rivals.

One of Joe Paterno's goals was to lead the Nittany Lions to the Rose Bowl, the only major bowl he had missed. All he had to do was win the Big Ten championship. So guess what? In only the Lions' second year in the league, they swept through their opponents in 1993 and gained a Rose Bowl berth for the first time since the 1922 season.

In their previous visit to the Rose Bowl, the Lions lost to Southern Cal 14-3. This time was different. Penn State beat Pac-10 champion Oregon 38-20 to complete a perfect 12-0 season.

Scoring points was no problem for this team. Led by the passing of Kerry Collins, the pass catching of Kyle Brady and Bobby Engram and the running of Ki-Jana Carter, the Lions broke 14 school records and led the nation in scoring and total offense.

Meanwhile, Paterno was on his way to another record: The all-time mark for coaching victories in Division 1-A. He finally reached that milestone with his record 324th in 2001 with a 29-27 victory over Ohio State.

A Matchless Coach

Joe Paterno's coaching achievements are hard to match. Getting his clothing to match is quite another achievement, say some of his players.

Asked before the 2002 season what people don't know about Paterno, Penn State defensive tackle Jimmy Kennedy told a reporter:

"What a crazy fashion sense he has. He's the only cat I know who will roll out of bed and put on royal-blue pants and a green sweater vest. We can tell as soon as he shows up to practice whether Sue [Paterno] was around to dress him that day or not. We bust his chops about his clothes all the time."

No Grand Illusion

When he took over Penn State football in 1966, Joe Paterno instituted the so-called "Grand Experiment" with the thought of integrating athletes into university life. The idea of a successful student athlete was foreign to many of the nation's top football programs at the time—and still is, in fact.

As far as Penn State defensive tackle Jimmy Kennedy was concerned, the "Experiment" has been simply grand in his own case.

"If not for Joe Paterno, who knows where I would be today," Kennedy said prior to the 2002 season. "I've been in and out of Special Ed classes since the 10th grade, and I made the dean's list last September. That's because of the Paternos, Joe and his wife, Sue. Mrs. Paterno would show up some nights at 11 o'clock to tutor me on vocabulary, literature, anything I had trouble with."

The "Experiment" has generated its share of both cynics and believers, and probably some jealousy as well. None can dispute at least one fact: An NCAA report for Division I schools in 2001 showed Penn State's football players had a four-year graduation rate that was quite a bit higher than the national average.

A Beaver Tale

They call it the "House That Paterno Built," and for good reason. Beaver Stadium has been moved once and expanded seven times in Joe Paterno's tenure as the Nittany Lions coach.

Capacity going into the 2002 season: 107,282, larger than any NFL stadium and second largest in the country only by a few hundred to the University of Michigan. When filled to capacity on game day, Beaver Stadium becomes Pennsylvania's third largest "city," behind only Philadelphia and Pittsburgh.

Beaver Stadium is a money machine, generating hundreds of millions of dollars for the university's other athletic programs as well as its libraries, dorms and research facilities.

But it was almost the "House That Didn't Get Built", if Paterno ever had his way.

Beaver Stadium was originally located on campus when a decision was made in the late 1950s to move it so that seats could be added. The long-range thinking was that perhaps 16,000 seats could be tacked on, bringing the capacity to 46,824.

The plan was to have the old stadium torn down after the 1959 season and reassembled on a new site close to campus. There was only one highly vocal dissenter: Paterno.

"Shows you how smart I was," Paterno said.

On game days Beaver Stadium becomes the third largest population center in Pennsylvania, behind Philadelphia and Pittsburgh.

Just Peachy

Having a stadium, street or even a sandwich named after you is a sure sign of celebrity on any college campus.

At Penn State, there's the Paterno Library, but it's not the only tribute to Joe Paterno.

There have been life-size cardboard cutouts of Paterno sold at various stores around campus, golf balls with Paterno's face on them and, believe it or not, an internet site for people who have named their pets after the Penn State coach.

Plus, Paterno has had BOTH a sandwich and an ice cream flavor named after him, in the best tradition of the Carnegie Deli in New York.

The sandwich? The "Sloppy Joepa," served at the Penn State Sub Shop at State College. The ingredients: a choice of meat—turkey, roast beef or ham—along with cole slaw and French fries. The cole slaw and fries are not served on the side, but rather piled high (presumably sloppily) on a roll of Italian bread.

And the ice cream? Why, "Peachy Paterno"—what else? That's available at the Penn State Creamery, a popular campus meeting place. Once on a visit to Penn State, President Clinton actually stopped by for a taste of "Peachy Paterno."

There was no word whether the Democratic president swung a vote his way from the Penn State coach, a registered Republican.

Against the Law

Joe Paterno, New York lawyer?

That isn't a flippant remark about Paterno's vocal style. At one time the Penn State coach was actually thinking about law school before accepting a coaching job at Penn State in 1950.

After playing football at Brown, where he was an English Lit major, Paterno was on his way to a career in law when the offer came from Rip Engle to join him at University Park. Engle was Paterno's coach at Brown.

"I was really flattered," Paterno recalled of Engle's offer to be a quarterback coach at Penn State. "We just finished spring practice at Brown. Rip called me in and said, 'Would you like to coach?' I was excited and said I would like to, but I would have to talk to my family."

That meant talking to his father. He wasn't sure what his dad would say. After all, he was counting on a law career for his son.

"My father was a big help to me," Paterno remembered in a 1986 newspaper interview. "As much as he wanted me to be a lawyer and as disappointed as he was for me getting into coaching, he said, 'You know what you want to do. I can't live your life for you.'"

The conversation with his father closed one door and opened another for Paterno.

"He made it easy for me," Paterno said. "If he had in any way pressured me I probably would have gone to law school.

"I don't know if I'd be a big-city lawyer. I might be a poor New York City lawyer."

Super Sophs

For the winningest coach in Division I-A football history, Joe Paterno didn't exactly have an auspicious start at Penn State.

In his first season as the Nittany Lions' head coach in 1966, he lost two of his first three games and finished with a mediocre 5-5 record.

When his second season began with a loss to Navy, Paterno started to have self-doubts.

"I had to find out for myself," he remembered in a 1986 newspaper interview. "Either you can do it or you can't do it. If you can't coach, go sell insurance or do something that you can do."

The turning point came the next week when Penn State played at Miami. The night before, Paterno bused the team to Pittsburgh. There the Nittany Lions practiced on a high school field.

The next morning, they were on a plane to Florida. It was September and still hot in Miami. So Paterno made sure his players stayed indoors in air-conditioned comfort until it was time to leave for the stadium.

Paterno added a wrinkle that shook up the team: He started 14 sophomores, all the players he had recruited himself.

The Nittany Lions proceeded to beat Miami, 17-8. After a two-point loss to UCLA the following week, those 14 sophomores of 1967 didn't lose another game in their entire Penn State careers.

With those Paterno recruits playing a major role, the Nittany Lions started a 31-game unbeaten streak that included perfect seasons in 1968 and 1969. And Joe Paterno no longer had self-doubts about his coaching, or his recruiting, ability.

There's No Patronizing Paterno

Joe Paterno doesn't mind voicing his opinion about most anything—from sports to city government at State College. Talking about himself is another matter.

During the course of one magazine interview, Paterno heard a question that made him chuckle. The question: "Do you use any bits and pieces from other great coaches in your style?"

Paterno looked at his interviewer with a twinkle in his eye.

"I'm glad to hear you say 'other great coaches,'" Paterno said.

Then he launched into a favorite story.

"There's this coach shaving himself in the mirror and saying to his wife, 'Do you know how many great coaches there are in this country?' And the wife says, 'One less than you think.'"

Paterno added his own punch line through a burst of laughter.

"I put myself in that 'one less' category."

A Higher Calling

It's two hours before game time and things are getting warmed up at Beaver Stadium. Not on the field, in the stands.

That's generally the time the fans usually spring into action with their cell phones, creating a logjam of calls in the vicinity.

"The largest spike [on phone calls] will occur an hour or two before game time," a Verizon Wireless spokesman said in an interview with The Associated Press. "I equate that to people trying to look for people at tailgates."

Hard to believe, but as many as 500,000 phone calls might be made before, during and after a Penn State football game. Although there are seven cellular phone towers near the stadium, sometimes it's not enough to handle the high volume of calls. In 2002 Beaver Stadium officially seated 107,252.

The cell phones usually not only sizzle with conversation, but "text messaging" as well, according to the Verizon spokesman. He speaks from personal experience.

During Penn State's game against Louisiana Tech, he contacted a Nittany Lion fan vacationing on Nantucket Island.

"We are" said his terse message.

"Penn State," came back the reply, completing the popular Nittany Lions chant.

Lionized

In the 2002-03 semester year at Penn State, more than a million people visited State College—more than 800,000 for football games alone. Safe to say many of them stopped by the "Nittany Lion," proud symbol of Penn State athletics.

Like a procession going to a religious shrine, visitors usually make their way to the leafy nook where the famed sculpture stands—or rather, crouches—right by old Recreation Hall.

The large, gold-colored lion carved by Heinz Warnneke out of limestone might be the most photographed spot on campus. Legend has it the lion once roamed nearby Mount Nittany, part of the Appalachian forest.

As for the mountain, there's another legend connected with that. It concerns Nita-Nee, an Indian princess beloved by her people for leading them to the fertile valley in central Pennsylvania now known as State College. When she died, a mountain rose up overnight over the place she was buried.

"Nita-Nee" eventually became "Nittany."

Tunnel Vision

The gun went off and the scoreboard at Beaver Stadium flashed the final tally: Miami 33, Penn State 7.

No matter. September 1, 2001 was already one of the greatest days in Penn State football history.

More important to many than the result flashed on the scoreboard after the game was what was flashed before the game:

"BELIEVE."

Adam Taliaferro had made believers of many that night when he led the Nittany Lions onto the field for the start of the nationally televised game, jogged past dozens of cameramen and waved to the roaring 109,313 fans in attendance.

A year earlier, there was little reason to believe Taliaferro would walk again, much less lead the Nittany Lions out of the tunnel for a game. That was the prognosis of many of his doctors after he suffered a severe spinal cord injury in a game at Ohio State.

The Nittany Lions' freshman cornerback was paralyzed while tackling Ohio State running back Jerry Westbrooks. The play with less than two minutes remaining hardly impacted the game—Penn State was on its way to a 45-6 loss.

But it impacted many lives. For one of the few times in his coaching career, Joe Paterno was practically speechless.

"As a coach," Paterno remembered, "it was my toughest week. It was a struggle not knowing how to handle the squad."

Taliaferro, meanwhile, was handling things a different way, through the power of positive thinking. He vowed to return to Penn State and lead the Nittany Lions through the tunnel onto the field for a game.

That would seem miraclous, considering his condition. Despite successful spinal fusion surgery, Taliaferro was completely immobile. Few doctors believed he would ever get out of a wheelchair. Some thought he was lucky to be alive.

Their thinking began to change, however, after Taliaferro went through a couple months of therapy at Magee Rehabilitation Hospital in Philadelphia. While his Penn State teammates were battling through a losing season, Taliaferro was winning little battles of his own with help from the superb Magee therapists.

Sensations began returning to his body one by one as he graduated from the bed to wheelchair to treadmill. Soon, he was able to walk with a crutch, then finally on his own, if a bit unsteadily. When he walked out of Magee under his own power, it was a much more exhilarating feeling than he ever had scoring touchdowns as a high school star in Philadelphia.

With the help of doctors, therapists, friends and family, Taliaferro had miraculously pulled through. It had been a year of tears and triumph while a nation prayed for him. Taliaferro had wanted to be a famous football player. Now he was famous, although it was hardly the way he expected.

He had been an inspiration to many wheelchair-bound people in America, not just athletes. His feel-good story had been embraced by an entire country.

Then emotions ran high at Beaver Stadium the night of Sept. 1, 2001. As Taliaferro led the Nittany Lions onto the field against Miami, a video on the scoreboard showed him sweating and grimacing through therapy over the winter.

Flashbulbs popped and cheers filled the stadium. For one game, at least, the result was irrelevant. Penn State already had its victory.

Pacing Paterno

Joe Paterno doesn't need a treadmill. He gets plenty of his walking exercise during a football game, thank you.

Anyone who has ever seen a Penn State game knows Paterno constantly paces up and down the sidelines—sometimes walking as much as four times as his team's total offense that day.

"There are a lot of things I've got to keep doing...a lot of people I've got to see and I've got to move back and forth where I can see the action best," Paterno says.

Joe Paterno prowling the sidelines. Sometimes his yardage total exceeded that of his team.

Contrary to some beliefs, the sidelines are not the best place to watch a football game. Paterno calls it the "worst seat in the house. You can see less from there than anywhere in the stadium."

That's why he relies heavily on assistant coaches in the press box, communicating with them by phone. It still doesn't stop him from his habitual pacing, though.

Ankle-Deep

In 1999, there was no doubt who was the best college linebacker in the country—Penn State's LaVar Arrington. His emotional style, though, went against the grain of normally conservative Penn State football.

Arrington, who won the Dick Butkus Award as the nation's top linebacker and the Chuck Bednarik Award as the country's top defensive player, celebrated big hits with a flourish and taunted his opponents unmercifully. This led to clashes with Penn State coaches who sometimes found Arrington as hard to contain as his opponents did.

Whether promoting himself as the top linebacker or patting Joe Paterno on the butt during team meetings, Arrington was as irrepressible as they come.

Paterno admitted that Arrington had "lots of personality" and gave him some room to express himself. But not too much. Once after running back an interception 16 yards for a touchdown against Bowling Green, Arrington did a high-stepping dance inside the pylon.

Paterno was not pleased, although Arrington offered this explanation:

"It was not a high-step. Their little quarterback was diving at my ankles."

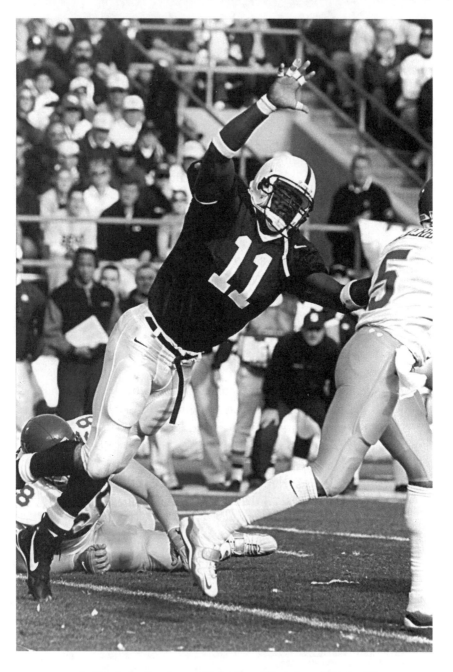

LaVar Arrington leaped into the national spotlight with his aggressive linebacker play at Penn State.

Leaping LaVar

In just two full seasons of varsity ball at Penn State, linebacker LaVar Arrington became a legend at a school known for turning out great linebackers.

Known for his athleticism, Arrington continually turned heads by leaping over the line to make tackles in the backfield. One such play, in which he stopped Illinois fullback Elmer Hickman for no gain on fourth and one to help preserve a shutout, is chronicled in Penn State lore as the "LaVar Leap."

Before making a name for himself as the best defensive player in the country, Arrington played sporadically as a freshman in 1997. It was still enough to impress opposing coaches. Penn State was playing Minnesota at home and Arrington was seeing action on the special teams squad.

"It was during a kickoff and I saw this No. 11 for Penn State running downfield and making the tackle and I thought to myself, 'Oh, God, what a great-looking athlete,'" recalled Golden Gophers coach Glen Mason in a 1999 interview. "So I said to him, 'Hey, you're the best-looking No. 11 in America.' And he just smiled."

The following season, Penn State was playing Minnesota in Minneapolis and Arrington made another spectacular tackle right in front of Mason.

"I said, 'Hey, Arrington, you're the best No. 11 in America,'" Mason said.

Arrington, usually never humble about his football talent, responded in typical fashion: "Oh, you know my name this year."

A Legitimate Request

Under assistant coach Jerry Sandusky, the Nittany Lions turned out some of the best defensive teams in college football.

Finally, after 32 years, the Nittany Lions' longtime defensive coordinator retired following the 2000 season. When he went out, Sandusky didn't leave a whole lot of talent for replacement Tom Bradley with which to work.

No less than nine defensive starters were lost to either the pros or graduation, including Courtney Brown and LaVar Arrington, the Nos. 1-2 picks in the 2000 NFL draft. It gave Bradley some reason to tease Sandusky.

"I don't mind you leaving," Bradley said, "but do LaVar and Courtney have to go, too?"

Ageless Joe

Joe Paterno's longevity as a coach at Penn State has been a source of amazement to many and a source of amusement to some.

Speculating in 2002 on who might replace Paterno, a sports writer suggested that his successor could very well be Fran Gantner, the longtime offensive coordinator at Penn State.

On second thought, maybe not, the sports writer added.

"He's 53," he said of Gantner. "By the time Paterno hits 120 and announces he'll go at least 10 more years, Gantner— a mere mortal—will be too old."

They Have a Point

The best team in Penn State football history? For openers, try either the great defensive squads of 1968 and 1969 that went 11-0, including a victory in the Orange Bowl each season. Or the 1973 team that carved out a 12-0 record with Heisman Trophy winner John Cappelletti.

Or how about the national champions of 1982 (11-1) and 1986 (12-0) or the 1978 team (11-1) that played for the title? Oldtimers might even suggest the 9-0-1 Penn State team in 1947 that went to the Cotton Bowl.

But for an offensive juggernaut, it would be hard to top the 1994 team. Led by quarterback Kerry Collins and tailback Ki-Jana Carter, the Nittany Lions scored 526 points for an average of 47.8 a game—both school records. Then after their 11-0 season, the Nittany Lions overwhelmed Oregon 38-20 in the Rose Bowl.

The 1982 team could put up a pretty good argument—and did while on a visit back to campus one weekend in 1994. Many of the members of Penn State's first national championship team had returned for homecoming weekend for the Ohio State game. Penn State was ranked No. 1 in the country at that point and Ohio State, No. 21.

"I think defensively we were probably a little better in '82," said Mark Battaglia, who played center. "Offensively, they're a little better...a lot better than we were in '82."

Asked how he felt the 1982 and 1994 teams would fare in a head-to-head battle, Battaglia said diplomatically, "I think it would probably be a draw. It would be co-national champions."

After which the 1994 Lions made quite a statement for themselves with a 63-14 pasting of Ohio State.

Comeback Kid

Kerry Collins got off to a forgettable start at Penn State. It would be hard to forget his finish.

Collins was supposed to be Penn State's starting quarterback in 1992, but was sidelined for most of the season by a fractured finger.

The following year, he missed spring practice after he was injured in a loss to Stanford in the Blockbuster Bowl. He then lost the starting QB job to John Sacca that fall. "I figured I'd be a backup for the rest of my career," Collins said.

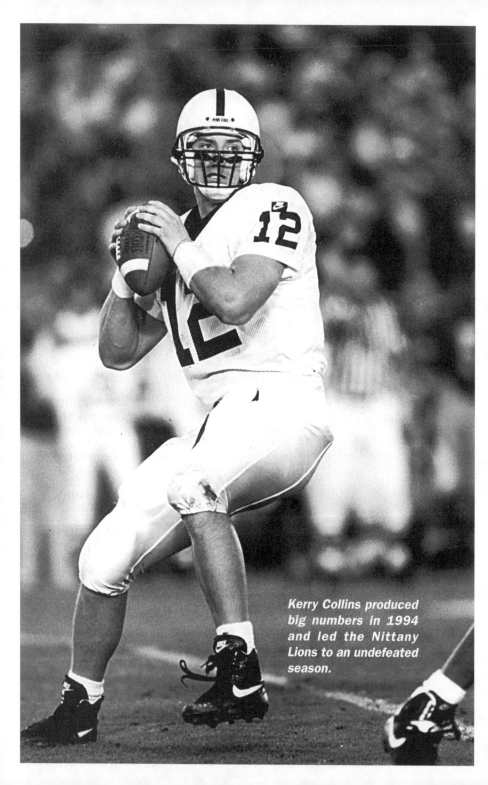

Kerry Collins produced big numbers in 1994 and led the Nittany Lions to an undefeated season.

That changed when Sacca was pulled early in the third game of the 1993 season against Iowa. Collins finished up a 31-0 victory. Sacca, incensed over being taken out of the game, abruptly left school two weeks later. Collins was suddenly the No. 1 quarterback, but things still weren't all that rosy for him.

Four weeks later, he had a terrible day in the mud and snow at Ohio Stadium. He only managed to complete 13 of 39 passes. Four of his passes were intercepted as Ohio State whipped the Lions, 24-6.

Collins was booed by Penn State fans. They were calling for Wally Richardson to replace him. These were basically the same fans that had cheered for Collins when he threw for 400 yards in the Blue-White game in the spring of 1992.

"You never want to lose hope," Collins said. "You always want to strive to be the best, but things weren't looking too good then."

They were looking better the rest of the season with five straight victories, including a decision over Tennessee in the Citrus Bowl. And better still in 1994, when Collins came of age. All of a sudden, he wasn't only the number-one quarterback at Penn State. He was number one in the nation.

Things were a little different when Ohio State visited Penn State that season. This time, Collins was unstoppable—and so was Penn State, in a 63-14 spanking of the Buckeyes.

In just their second season in the Big Ten, the Nittany Lions won every game and finished the year with a resounding victory over Oregon in the Rose Bowl. They were ranked No. 2 in the country.

Collins had the greatest single-season performance by a Penn State quarterback—completing nearly 67 percent of his passes for 2,679 yards. And the Nittany Lions had their greatest offensive season.

Another note of significance: Collins finished fourth in the voting for the Heisman Trophy.

Despite the early setbacks, Collins was patient, had worked hard and kept the faith.

"Do that," he said, "and usually good things happen."

Kerry at the Controls

During the 1994 season, it was usually lights out for Penn State's opponents. But when the Nittany Lions fell behind Illinois 21-0 in the first quarter of their game at Champaign, it looked pretty dark for them.

In 337 previous games under Joe Paterno, the Lions had never come back to win from such a deficit. It wouldn't be any easier against a defense that was rated No. 4 in the country.

It would take a tremendous performance by quarterback Kerry Collins and the Lions to pull it out. That's what they got.

Collins finally got the Lions untracked with a 99-yard TD drive. Still, it was 28-14 Illinois at the half, and Penn State was in danger of having its winning streak stopped at 13.

Things started to turn for Penn State in the second half, though. Collins guided another drive that finished with Ki-Jana Carter scoring to bring the Nittany Lions within seven points. Back came Illinois with a field goal.

The teams went into the fourth quarter with Penn State trailing 31-21.

But not for long.

With a fourth and one on the Illinois 32-yard line, Collins fired a 17-yard pass to Bobby Engram. That set up a five-yard touchdown run by Brian Milne.

Illinois still led late in the fourth quarter, 31-28, and was driving for the clinching TD. Time for the Penn State defense to step up. The Nittany Lions, led by Brian Gelzheiser, held and forced the Illini to punt.

That put the ball on the Penn State four. Time was running out on the Nittany Lions. Ninety-six yards to go for pay dirt. Everyone in the stadium figured that Penn State would have to pass if it hoped to win.

It didn't mean the Illini could stop Collins, however.

He merely completed seven of seven passes for 60 yards in one of the most masterful performances of clock management ever seen at Penn State. And Milne smashed over from the 2 with 57 seconds left for a 35-31 Penn State lead.

There was still time for Illinois to come back. Again, the Illini was driving for a score when Kim Herring intercepted a pass in the end zone as the final gun sounded.

Along with the greatest comeback of his career, there were other firsts for Paterno—Penn State's first Big 10 title and the first time he had taken the Nittany Lions to the Rose Bowl. It had probably aged him a little, though, to watch that heart-stopping Illinois game go down to the wire.

Against All Odds

When Penn State defensive tackle Chris Mazyck scored a touchdown against Ohio State in 1994, it was meaningless as far as the game was concerned. Not so for Chris himself.

Measured in human elements, the TD by Mazyck far overshadowed Penn State's 63-14 win that day. And for many in the crowd of 97,079 on Homecoming Day at University Park, it was also a meaningful moment.

Five years earlier, Mazyck had entered Penn State as a hotshot recruit after winning high school Player of the Year honors in South Carolina. His future seemed bright. His outlook quickly changed while on a visit home to Columbia during spring break in 1991.

Mazyck was shot six times in his left leg by a man with a .45 revolver when he refused to let his sister date him. Damage was so extensive to the leg that doctors feared he would lose it.

Somehow the leg was saved. Saving his football career was another matter. At the time all Joe Paterno and his staff could hope for was that Mazyck would walk again.

The leg was immobile for eight months. "They gave me a lot of support and told me not to worry about football," Mazyck said.

Mazyck didn't worry. All he did was work out. And, remarkably, two years after the incident he managed to return to the team for the 1993 season.

Mazyck had seemingly worked a miracle just by stepping back onto a football field. Soon enough, he was doing more than that as he got more and more playing time each game. Against Michigan State in the final game of the season, he burst through the line for two key sacks that lifted the Nittany Lions to a comeback victory.

As a fifth-year senior, it would be his last game at Penn State. Or would it?

At the end of the 1993 season, Penn State petitioned the NCAA to grant Mazyck an extra year of eligibility. It wasn't something the NCAA ordinarily did. But considering Mazyck's unusual circumstances, the NCAA granted a sixth year of eligibility for Penn State's courageous lineman.

So you could understand the riotous reaction from many Penn State fans when Mazyck scored the TD against Ohio State on an interception return.

"The whole play felt like it took about 30 minutes," Mazyck once recalled. "I think it took about three seconds for the ball to get into my hands once it was tipped. I was surprised when the ball landed in my hands. I stared at it for a while before I ran."

Mazyck knew exactly where he wanted to go, however.

"I don't think an army could have held me back," he said.

The Finishing Touch

It was the 2001 season and a frustrated Penn State team was facing yet another defeat. Only 1:39 remained in the game at Northwestern and the Nittany Lions trailed 35-31 with the ball on their own 48-yard line.

Even more ominous: the Lions had lost two of their top offensive players to injury, quarterback Matt Senneca and tailback Larry Johnson.

It seemed a probability that Penn State would lose its fifth straight to start the season, a shocking scenario. And once more, Joe Paterno would be denied the opportunity to tie Bear Bryant on the all-time coaches victory list.

Enter Zach Mills. What could the backup quarterback say to his team as he entered the huddle in an almost hopeless situation?

How about: "What's up, fellas? I missed y'all. You ready to take this in?"

That was Mills—cool as a fall morning in State College.

Mills had been a redshirt freshman and spent most of his sophomore season as a backup to Senneca, seeing action only when the top quarterback was hurt.

True, Mills had been a big prep school star in Maryland, leading his Urbana High School team to consecutive state championships in 1998 and 1999. And he had made a strong collegiate debut against Miami after an injury to Senneca. But did anyone expect this 19-year-old QB, largely untested in big-time college football, to lead a Lions comeback on enemy ground with less than two minutes remaining and 52 yards to go?

Mills did.

Needing no less than a touchdown, Mills accomplished just that. He completed five of eight passes for 54 yards, including a four-yard TD toss to Eric McCoo with 22 seconds

Zach Mills: A habit of heroism in big games.

left for the winning score. Final: Penn State 38, Northwestern 35. Just like in the movies.

Nor did his heroics stop there. Comebacks and a confident demeanor became a Mills trademark. He also rallied Penn State to remarkable comeback victories over Ohio State and Michigan State coming off the bench in 2001. By 2002, Senneca had graduated and Mills had firmly established himself as the Lions' number-one quarterback.

Now he could start games as well as finish them.

Like Father, Like Son: Really

College football history is replete with stories of sons who followed in their fathers' footsteps by playing at the same school.

But how many can boast of matching their father's accomplishment of playing on a college team with a perfect record?

Meet Tony Pittman, son of former Penn State great Charlie Pittman.

Charlie Pittman was a top running back for Penn State's unbeaten, untied teams in 1968 and 1969. Both those squads went 11-0 and finished No. 2 in the wire service rankings.

Tony Pittman was a standout safety on Penn State's 1994 team that finished 12-0 and also No. 2 in the national rankings. He honored his father by wearing a uniform with the same number, 24.

Those aren't the only coincidences in the Pittman family story.

Strangely enough, both father and son made their starting debuts against West Virginia in the midst of some Penn State setbacks.

For Charlie Pittman, it was 1967 when Paterno put him in against the Mountaineers. The Lions had lost two of their first four games. Twenty-five years later, Tony made his first start at West Virginia after two straight losses by the Nittany Lions.

The result?

"We won, and so did my dad's team," Tony Pittman said. Obviously. It was in the genes.

Uniformly Together

The National Football League's "Throwback Weekend" set up the perfect punch line for Penn State offensive tackle Keith Conlin during the 1994 season.

Referring to the pros' occasional practice of wearing classic, old-time uniforms as a tribute to the past, Conlin quipped, "We'd have a throwback day every week."

His reference, of course, was to the plain blue and white uniforms worn by the Nittany Lions for as long as anyone could remember. The "plain vanilla" uniforms have been derided by some, but mostly held in reverence by the Penn State players for their pure simplicity.

When coach Joe Paterno once approached the team about putting patches on the uniforms to mark college football's 125th anniversary, he was wholeheartedly rejected.

Paterno had to chuckle.

"[Offensive lineman Bucky] Greeley told me it's bad enough they have to wear that Nike logo so you and your wife can get a free trip every year," Paterno said. "He really gave me the business."

Actually, the concession to wear the "swoosh" Nike logo was made to bring in extra money for other sports programs. An added bonus: shoes and various sideline apparel.

Aw, Cut It Out

True story: A teenager in Clinton, Pennsylvania, saw a silhouette in a window of a vacationing neighbor's house.

Shaken, he called the cops. It looks like an intruder, he nervously told them.

Police quickly arrived to find that the "intruder" was nothing more than a stand-up, cardboard cutout of Joe Paterno.

The life-size cutout is one of the hottest items sold at State College.

Bowling Them Over

The unbridled long-term success of the Penn State football program makes some forget about the struggles that Joe Paterno had at the beginning, first as an assistant coach and then as head coach.

"When I came here with Rip Engle, he had a tough job on his hands," Paterno remembered. "We had to work hard to get kids to come."

It was 1950 when Engle and Paterno, his young, untested coaching assistant, first arrived at State College from Brown. There was nothing remarkable about the Penn State teams in those early years. Getting top players was tough then for the Nittany Lions, as Paterno remembered.

"We used to go out to Western Pennsylvania and sometimes we couldn't get a visit out of a kid," he said. "When we went east, we had trouble getting kids Penn wanted."

Both Engle and Paterno worked hard on recruiting and eventually got things turned around. It did take them the better part of the 50s to do it, though. It was 10 years before one of Engle's teams landed a bowl berth. They were 3-1 in such games before Engle handed the head coaching reins over to Paterno in 1966.

A pride of Lions at Beaver Stadium. Nothing's changed over the years, not even the uniforms.

Since then, bowl visits have been a habit at Penn State. Going into the 2003 season, Paterno was the all-time leader in bowl victories with 20.

Where's Joe? Over There, on the Sidelines

It was 1993, Penn State's inaugural football season in the Big Ten. There was excitement everywhere, and not only at State College.

Everywhere the Nittany Lions played, there was more than the usual interest from opposing teams. All because of the legendary aura of Joe Paterno.

When Illinois played the Nittany Lions for the first time since 1972, the game wasn't the only thing on the minds of the Illini players.

"Everybody was looking for Joe Paterno," Illinois linebacker Dana Howard said. "In the huddle, everybody was asking, 'Where's Joe? Where's Joe?' He's a legend."

Not that it was a distraction. But Penn State did whip the Illini that day, 28-14.

Not All in the Same Family

When Joe Paterno called out "Johnson" during the 2002 season, it caused heads to turn—sometimes as many as seven.

No less than six players and one coach shared the same last name on that year's Nittany Lion team. The only players related, however, were senior tailback Larry Johnson and his brother, Tony, a junior wide receiver. Their father, Larry, Sr., served as Penn State's defensive line and punting coach.

In addition, the other Johnsons included: Bryant, a senior wide receiver; Donnie, a freshman running back; Ed, a freshman defensive lineman, and Tim, a sophomore linebacker.

Repositioning Himself

As an assistant coach at Penn State, Larry Johnson Sr. had the opportunity to see a lot of his football-playing sons. That wasn't always the case when Larry and Tony were growing up and Johnson was coaching high school football in Maryland.

The elder Johnson was a workaholic, spending long hours breaking down game films and running practices and staff meetings. He rarely got home in time to put his kids to bed.

Then something happened that caused him to change his schedule. One day Tony's kindergarten teacher called. Tony was asked to talk about his parents.

"My mom's name is Christine Johnson," Tony said. "My father's name is Coach."

That's when Johnson knew he had been spending too much time at the office.

Mind Set

When he played at Penn State, Larry Johnson wanted to be known as the "nastiest, most craziest back ever." It was all part of Johnson's preparation for games. He felt he had to be mean-spirited, even in team practices, in order to succeed as a running back.

When Johnson was kicked out of practice for fighting with teammates from time to time, nobody raised an eyebrow. That was just Johnson being, well, Johnson. For years, Penn State players were used to the scowl on his face. It didn't make Johnson any happier when he had to share the running load with two other tailbacks—Omar Easy and Eric McCoo.

Finally, as a senior in 2002, Johnson was designated as the number one running back in the Nittany Lions' offense.

Easy and McCoo were gone. Teammates noticed then that Johnson was starting to smile a little.

Why?

"I finally have a job," Johnson said.

Johnson was smiling even more when he became the first back at Penn State to rush for more than 2,000 yards in a season. Baseball legend Leo Durocher, who coined the phrase "Nice guys finished last," probably would have loved this guy.

It Grew on Him

Charming as it is, Penn State's campus isn't always love at first sight for everyone. Ironically, it wasn't for Joe Paterno.

"Rip Engle brought Joe in as an assistant in 1950," remembered onetime athletic director Jim Tarman. "And when Joe, who was from Brooklyn, got his first look at State College, he told Rip, 'I'll stay here for one year, but after that you'll have to get yourself another boy.'"

Paterno only missed the length of his stay at Penn State by more than 50 years.

Nittany Lions Face Lift

When Penn State unveiled an assortment of new logos in 1996, including a fiercer looking Nittany Lion, Joe Paterno was pleased.

"It looks mean," Paterno said of the fresh illustration of the Nittany Lion. "I kinda like it."

Not that Paterno was ready to put the logo on the Penn State uniform. He said he preferred that the uniform remain plain as usual.

"But I may put it on my Jockey shorts," Paterno quipped.

A Family Affair

A senior's last football game at home is usually filled with plenty of emotion. That went triple for the Johnson family on Nov. 23, 2002 when Penn State played Michigan State.

It was Larry Johnson's final game at Beaver Stadium, the last time he would be on the same home field with his brother, Tony, and his father, Larry, Sr., Penn State's defensive line coach.

When Larry's name was announced along with the other upperclassmen on Senior Day, Tony hugged his brother and cried.

"I basically told him this is the last time we're going to play together," said Tony, a wide receiver. "It was kind of emotional. When we hugged, you could feel the brotherly love."

Later, Larry Johnson felt the emotion of fatherly love. When he scored the last of his four touchdowns of the day, his father was waiting on the sidelines to congratulate him.

"I just said, 'I love you, you did a great job,'" Larry Sr. said. "At the moment, it's just father-son talking. It's a special moment. I was trying very hard to hold back the tears, because I knew somebody would be taking a picture."

Johnson made his final game at Beaver Stadium memorable in other ways. He rushed for 279 yards—all in the first half—to become the first Penn State runner to gain more than 2,000 yards in a season. The Nittany Lions also had a big day as a team, whipping the Spartans 61-7.

Hot Ticket

Think it's easy being Joe Paterno? Not always—especially if you're actually not the Penn State football coach.

In 1997 a total of 17 Joe Paternos other than the famous JoePa were found in a national search by the *Harrisburg Pa-*

triot. And most of them had a story to tell regarding their name.

One Joe Paterno was a 55-year-old former long-haul truck driver who had been living on disability in Tampa, Florida. This Joe Paterno recalled the time he was stopped for speeding in Pennsylvania.

"My name still didn't get me out of a ticket," he said. "All they did was ask *me* if I could get tickets —to the football games."

A Snap for Joe

Meeting the media prior to the first game of the 1998 season, Joe Paterno was spelling out a laundry list of concerns —the defense, key injuries, etc. The big mystery, though, was the starting quarterback position.

Even though just a couple of days away from the game against Southern Mississippi, Paterno still wasn't sure who would start—senior Kevin Thompson or junior Rashad Casey. He said he might use both.

But reporters pressed Paterno on the issue. Paterno, a onetime quarterback, finally said he might take the snaps himself.

"In fact, I've got a year of eligibility left," quipped the 71-year-old Paterno who was then in his 33rd season as Penn State's head coach.

A Major Step Up

One of Joe Paterno's closest friends in the coaching business has been Johnny Majors. Once Majors left archrival Pitt after 1976, that is.

Paterno and Majors and their wives made a number of offseason trips to coaching clinics together. "We found we had a lot in common," Majors said.

Once on a trip to the Virgin Islands, Paterno's luggage was late in arriving. So Paterno wore Majors's clothes for three days. Majors was known as one of the sharpest dressers in the business.

"We wore the same size shoes [11C], the same waist and length pants and the same coat and shirt size," Majors said. "He told me he was the best dressed he had ever been."

He Has a Point

It was the summer of 2002 and coaches were gathered in Chicago for the annual Big Ten Media Day. Things hadn't changed—Joe Paterno was looking forward to another season and his colleagues continued to be in awe of his accomplishments.

Minnesota coach Glen Mason was one of them. He remembered that he had the recent pleasure of presenting to Paterno the Amos Alonzo Stagg Award for coaching excellence. Stagg, of course, was one of football's legendary early giants.

"I found it kind of humorous when I was looking through some numbers," Mason said, referring to Paterno's record victory total. "After a while, I thought maybe I should be giving the Joe Paterno Award to Amos Alonzo Stagg."

InnerWorkings™

INNERWORKINGS SALUTES
THE NITTANY LIONS!

1222 N. KINGSBURY • SUITE 202 • CHICAGO, IL 60622

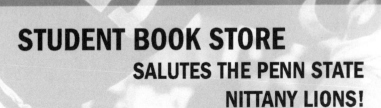